Those Crazy Germans!

Those Crazy Germans!

A Lighthearted Guide to Germany

Steven Somers

To order additional copies of this book, contact:
Xlibris Corporation
1-888-795-4274
www.Xlibris.com
Orders@Xlibris.com
34601

Contents

Dedication

To my wife, Danielle, my family, and my friends for indulging my love of all things German.

I have often been teased for being like the father in the movie *My Big Fat Greek Wedding*, who could always find a connection between any fact or word to Greek or Greece. Similarly, I, of course, can seemingly always find a connection with Germany. I hope this book proves that I wasn't making all of that stuff up!

Introduction:
Willkommen!

Welcome to Germany, the land of Beethoven and Bach, beer and bratwurst, BMWs and Benzes. Sure these are the typical images that may go through one's head when thinking about the Fatherland, but Germany is so much more, and Germans, traditionally known more for their *Ordnung* (order) than their capriciousness, are a surprisingly crazy *Volk* (people). *Those Crazy Germans!* provides an amusing (and sometimes irreverent) look into the lighter and lesser-known side of German culture and life (yes, there is one!).

Germany is a country steeped in tradition, rich in culture and history, and vibrant in its everyday activities. My aim is to help explain, and put into perspective, some of the uniqueness of Germans to travelers. I have had the good fortune to experience Germany up close and personal. At varying times I have lived, studied, worked in, as well as traveled throughout this remarkable country. For me, Germany is my second home. Although I'm not a German, I feel comfortable and right at home in the German culture, so much so, that I have killed-off many a cocktail party conversation with my tales of the Vaterland. Part of this simply stems from my fascination with the country; the other part from my dismay that Germans and their culture are generally underappreciated by my countrymen, with outdated stereotypes dominating most impressions. I hope this book unearths some of the harder to see gems of German society and culture. By providing you with some insight into how Germans behave, work, and play—in other words, how they live, I hope to enhance your trip. Germans are a lot more fun than they may seem at first glance and I hope that you'll discover your own *crazy* impressions of Germany and the Germans.

This book should be used as a companion guide to the many traditional guidebooks that list all the necessary elements for your stay, such as places to see, museums, restaurants and accommodations. *Those Crazy Germans!* does not attempt to supplant such guides, but rather offer some insight into common behavior in the BRD (Bundesrepublik Deutschland). So whether you are researching your trip, getting a few pointers while you sit on the plane or just trying to comprehend different cultural nuances, *Those Crazy Germans!* will hopefully shed some light on the subject.

I hope you enjoy your trip to Deutschland (either in the physical sense or the armchair one) and hope that you too will come to see Germans in a lighter fashion.

Gute Reise! (Roughly translated as "Happy Trails")

Teutonphile's Tip: Throughout the book you will find shaded text boxes entitled "Teutonphile's Tip". What exactly is a Teutonphile, you ask? A Teutonphile, in this case the author, is a lover of the Teutons, which is a term used to refer to Germanic people in general. Teutonphile's tips are quick pointers and suggestions to help you during your trip.

Chapter 1

What's in a Name:
It's All German to Me

The German language is a very structured and logical language and this, naturally, extends to the names of German cities, towns and places. Let's go over some basic German place-naming conventions which will help you better understand the origin of the town name and give you a peek into the history of the place.

Perhaps the most common naming convention you'll encounter is the word 'burg'. The word 'Burg' in German means 'fort' or 'fortress' and there are countless towns that either were forts or contained forts and that is where the town derived its name. Think of Pittsburgh as your American equivalent, which took its name from being the location of Fort Pitt. So towns like Duisburg, Regensburg, Augsburg, Rothenburg, Ravensburg, Freiburg, Würzburg, Meersburg and Hamburg all took their names from some association with a fort or fortress. This is not to be confused with the famous tourist town of Heidelberg. In Heidelberg's case, although a large castle dominates the town, the spelling here is 'berg', which means mountain or hill, and reflects the town's situation on the side of a mountain. The Bavarian town of Bamberg is another such example. Other common town names contain the word 'Bad', which simply means 'bath' and stems from the town having thermal springs at that location, most commonly settled by the Romans. Examples include the luxurious resort town of Baden-Baden to Bad Homburg near Frankfurt and Bad Godesberg, a part of the city of Bonn. Other common, yet less frequent, naming conventions include the word 'au', which means 'meadow' for the names of such places as Passau, Zwickau and Dessau, as well as 'Hafen' meaning harbor or port as in Ludwigshafen and Bremerhaven in the north and Friedrichshafen in the south.

Not every German place name has such ordinary origins like those already mentioned. Rather there are many names which reflect very unique heritages. Stuttgart, for example, means 'stud-garden' because Stuttgart was once the site of pastures where horses were put out to stud. This also explains why Stuttgart-based Porsche's logo contains the image of a horse. Sitting on the Isar River, the city of München was once an important location along the salt trade route to the Alps. However it was named for some monks who built a church at this location As such the name is derived from the word *Mönch* or Monk, and literally means 'of the Monks'. Karlsruhe, which sits on the Rhine River near the French border, got its name from the Margrave of Baden, named Karl Wilhelm, who during a hunting expedition took a rest or *Ruhe* at this location, and liked it so much that he constructed a grand palace and designed a city at this spot. The city of Berlin is associated with the word for bear or *Bär*, which explains why the city's coat of arms contains a bear. This is consistent with the Swiss capital of Bern, also connected with the bear. The town of *Bacharach*, perched on the Rhine River and dominated by the fort, *Burg Stahleck* (now a hostel), derives its name from Bachus, the Roman god of wine, and reflects the town's location in the heart of the Rheinland wine-growing region.

Coats of arms for the cities of Berlin, Munich and Stuttgart all depict the origins of their names

Given that much of Germany was once part of the Roman Empire, many names are derived from their Roman roots, such as Colonia for Köln, Confluentes (because it's at the confluence of the Rhein, Main and Mosel rivers) for Koblenz, Bavaria for Bayern and even Germania for Germany. This helps explain why the names are different in English than in German.

With these basic naming clues, it is possible to figure out a little bit of history about the town without having to get a history lesson. By doing so, you can begin to appreciate what makes that particular place interesting and it may help you decide whether to make a stop or not.

Chapter 2

Hotels and Restaurants:
Customs & Quirks

Since you will undoubtedly need some place to eat and sleep, there are a few customs and quirks that you should be aware of in Germany's hospitality industry. Being the do-it-yourselfers that the Germans are, the first thing you need to know about eating out is that you need to seat yourself. With rare exception, when entering a German restaurant or *Gasthaus*, a hostess will not greet you. Hence, don't stand around waiting for someone to come by and direct you to a table; it is the norm that you seat yourself. Simple enough, right? Well, almost right. If you are in a crowded or popular place, you may encounter signs on the tables. Some may read *Stammtisch*, which means this is a table for the restaurant's regulars. This, in and of itself, does not mean that you can't sit there, but if you do, you should be aware that you could draw ire from the regulars, or, if the regulars are friendly and not averse to your presence, be prepared to fully participate in the conversation. Other tables may indicate that they are reserved with a small card indicating for which times that table is reserved. If you are there comfortably before the reserved time, pull up a seat; otherwise keep moving. If the place is really jumping and you can't find an empty table for yourself, simply ask to join a table that has seats available. The phrase, *Ist dieser Platz frei?* (Is this seat free?) works best. Unless it happens to be couple on a romantic evening out or a very intimate group, you will most likely be welcomed without question. In some ways, not having a host is preferable because you don't have to stand around, and it can make the dining experience a bit more casual.

Once you get a seat, particularly at outdoor beer gardens, you may have to get up, wash your own beer mug, fill it at the tap, and then get a tray and serve yourself at the cafeteria-style serving area. While the idea of washing your mug isn't very appealing, it sounds much worse than it really is, and actually can add to the whole beer garden experience.

In their personal lives, Germans typically have an aversion to purchasing things on credit. Although the use of credit cards is on the rise in Germany, most *Deutscher* still pay for meals with cash when eating out. This preference for using cash for most daily transactions is best summed up by the German phrase, *"Nur Bar ist wahr"*, which translates, as "Only cash is real", but we understand it more as "Cash is King". As a result, waiters and waitresses carry around large amounts of Euro bills and coins for making change at the table when the time comes to pay. The use of cash is appreciated and also expedites your exit when you're in a hurry. Another nice perk in Germany is that it is customary for waiters and waitresses to provide separate bills. You will be asked if you would like to pay *"zusammen oder getrennt"*—together or separate, which is particularly useful when you are among friends, as it helps avoid the issue of who paid too much and who paid too little into the kitty.

Many German restaurants, particularly the cozy, middle-class establishments that serve hearty, traditional fare place baskets of pretzels or various breads and rolls on the table. These are neither gratis nor included in the price of the meal; they are extras. Germany is generally a very honest society, and if you snack on any of these items the waiter will ask you when tallying your bill if you have eaten any. If yes, they won't cost you more than a Euro or two, but be sure to be upfront about any of your noshing. Service in restaurants is pretty quick and reliable, if not always friendly. In Germany, the wait-service profession is a career for many and they take it seriously. Drinks are brought fresh and frequently, and servers make it their duty to ensure that you never have to wait long between beverages. Unlike American restaurants, water is usually not brought out unless specifically requested. Moreover, Germans have a penchant for sparkling mineral water, so be sure to request water, *ohne Gas*, or without carbonation, if you prefer still water. Furthermore, water will cost you a few Euros and will be tacked onto your bill. In the land of liquid gold, water is as costly as beer is, so don't be shocked when you get your bill, although most restaurants will have prices clearly marked on the menu.

> **Teutonphile's Tip:** As far as tipping goes don't be one of the millions of sucker tourists who have dropped tips of 10-20% on top of the bill. Customary tipping in Germany is to round up to the next whole Euro (i.e. If your bill is €24.20, you'd leave €25), which is a much more appropriate tip level.

Like much of Europe, Germany is a collection of regions and each region has its own dialect along with its own regional food specialties. Because of this, there are often different and unfamiliar names for foods on many restaurant menus. It is not uncommon for northern Germans to not know what some of the southern delicacies are and vice versa. This is widely understood, so if something on the menu is not translated into English, or is completely unfamiliar to you, don't be afraid to ask for an explanation. Some of the best items on the menu are the local specialties and you won't want to miss out simply because of a regional dialect issue.

The fact that Germans are a meat and potatoes kind of *Volk* is well-known. What is less known is that this begins at breakfast. *Frühstück*, as it's called, is a sort of quasi breakfast-lunch, but you can't quite call it brunch. A true German breakfast will consist of an assortment of cold cuts, cheeses and spreadable pâtés to go with the classic German roll, the *Semmel-Brötchen*. In addition, there is a variety of fruits to accompany one of the highlights of breakfast, the soft-boiled egg, which are served in a basket of carefully wrapped, cloth napkins. Placed in eggcups, the proper method for eating such an egg is to take your knife and decapitate the top the egg. By doing so you reveal the warm, gooey yoke in the middle, which you then dip your pieces of rye, pumpernickel, and multi-grain breads. German breakfast also usually includes *Müsli* and its own very special concoction called Quark, which is curd cheese, similar to cottage cheese. *Frühstück* is usually accompanied by coffee, teas steeped at your table, and a variety of fruit juices. It would be unfair to compare a German breakfast to an American farmer's breakfast, but it certainly is not your typical Continental breakfast of croissants and coffee. In Bavaria, breakfast is an even more robust affair consisting of a couple of boiled white sausages, called *Weisswürste*, that are washed down with a half-liter of the finest *Weissbier*. These sausages are very delicate and light on the palette, and there is nothing like a wheat-beer to start your day. Truth-be-told, this is not typically breakfast but a mid-morning snack for the Bavarians, but it certainly highlights how ingrained beer and sausages are in German culture.

Hotels have their own unique quirks too. In many family-run hotels, particularly outside the big cities, old habits die hard. In days of old, innkeepers would keep hold of the room keys when guests were out of the hotel. To remind guests to turn in their keys before leaving, keys were saddled with overly-large—and heavy, room number tags. The big key still exists at many hotels throughout Germany, and the principle still works because nobody wants to lug a half-pound key around. There is another very practical point about the big key. As there is no knob on the inside door handle to lock the door the only way to lock your hotel room door is to do so from the inside using the key. As hotels upgrade to the latest keycard technology the Big Key is going the way of the dodo, but make sure you when you lock the door you leave the key in the lock. Otherwise, you could have a problem if you need to get out of the room in a hurry.

Teutonphile's Tip: Try to stay at smaller family-operated hotels, guesthouses and Pension rather than at bigger, international chains of hotels. You'll get warm service and a real feel for German Gemütlichkeit (coziness and hospitality). You may not get a mini-bar in that room, but you shouldn't need to raid that fridge to get your fill of booze in Germany!

Lavatories in Germany have their own peculiarities as well. Because Germans are so environmentally conscious, they often have double-flush toilets. These toilets don't flush twice, but actually have an option for a big flush or a little flush. Water use remains a key component of Germany's conservation efforts, and this option allows the toilet user to exercise his environmentally conscientious attitude even in the most persnickety way. Along these same lines, Germans don't want you to linger too long in the shower either. To combat this, most showers have the shower half-wall. Instead of a shower-curtain or a full-length glass wall, Germans have given you the swinging half-length wall. The half-wall sits along the side of the shower or bathtub, theoretically to help keep water from spraying out of the tub. However, since it is only half-length and doesn't seal entirely along the tub, the water inevitably ends up on the floor. I've never quite figured out why they don't put in full-length shower curtains, but I'm sure there is some very good German reason for it.

Paying to Go

Public restrooms in Germany are a bit of an oddity. Whether in a train station, a beer hall or a park facility, the use of the restroom or WC is not without cost. Some more modern facilities charge a Euro or two just to get through the turnstiles, while others don't have any barriers. But that doesn't mean it's free. Almost without exception, these facilities are tended to by little, old ladies who leave out a small plate where patrons can leave their payment. Customary payment is usually 50 cents to a Euro and is a great way to unload that small change that tends to accumulate in your pockets. If you are a man, and you are relieving yourself, it can be somewhat unsettling that these bathroom attendants or Klofrau (Klo is the German slang for "john"), are walking around behind you cleaning the floors or even the urinal next to you! Don't be alarmed, this is par for the course and completely normal in Germany. It may seem odd to pay for the privilege of going, but it's a small price to pay.

Chapter 3

Rules, Rules and More Rules:
Is this allowed?

At heart, Germans are a people that live and die by rules. Sure, we Americans have our fair share of statutes, ordinances, regulations and rules, but Germans have the gig down to a science. Germany's affinity for rules and regulations is probably a deep-seated cultural issue that goes back hundreds of years and reflects their desire for order and efficiency, all of which may be rooted in Germany's feudalistic origins and later reinforced by the Kaiser and then the Nazis. All you really need to know is that theirs is a culture that places a high value on having and more importantly, obeying rules. As such, you should be aware that if you commit an infraction for something like, God forbid, crossing the street without the proper signal, an ordinary citizen may reprimand you. This is no joke. I once had to talk my way out of a street crossing violation after being flagged by the Polizei. This is becoming less of an issue as the younger generation is also more likely to flaunt the rules themselves.

A Matter of Timing

Germany's retail stores are subject to the country's *Ladenschlußgesetz* or "store-closing law", which sets the times when stores must close. Prior to 1996, stores had only limited operating hours. After heated debate, the law was changed to allow stores to remain open until 8 p.m. on weekdays and until 4 p.m. on Saturdays. This was a dramatic change for Germans and went to the core of German living and society's high value on personal time. Due to societal changes, the law has been relaxed further to allow for 24 hour a day opening times. However, old habits die hard and many stores have kept the

Still, Germans seem to enjoy reprimanding rule-breakers and self-policing is common. In the interest of not giving yourself or your fellow countrymen a bad name, you should try to stay within the parameters of the law which, with a little common sense, is easily accomplished. I certainly don't want to give you the impression that Germany is a police state—far from it. Germany's *Grundgesetz*, or Basic Law, is similar to the U.S. Constitution in form and function, and given its history, freedoms are held dearly in the BRD. That being said, Germany prides itself on its ability to be efficient, and a law-abiding citizenry is critical to maintaining this efficiency. The general rule of thumb in Germany is that nothing is permitted unless explicitly indicated, as opposed to the other way around in the U.S.

old opening times in place. More important, except for a handful of Sundays during the year, shops must still remain closed on Sundays. This is something to be particularly aware of if you are spending just a weekend and want to shop as well. Sightseeing venues are usually open on Sundays, but stores aren't, so plan accordingly. So something as seemingly simple as determining your own store hours is even regulated in the BRD.

Chapter 4

Highways and Byways:
Life in the Fast Lane

Most things in Germany are designed for efficiency. Nowhere is that more self-evident than in the country's network for transportation and travel. If a casual, relaxed mode of travel is what you seek, I suggest you head on down to one of the Mediterranean countries, where the pace is just a bit more leisurely. If it is speed, punctuality and efficiency that you prefer then you've come to the right place. In a nutshell, that describes the situation in Germany. If you are accustomed to America's systems of public transportation, highways and more modest speeds, you're going to need to raise your standards just a bit.

Let's start with the famed Autobahn. The Autobahn itself is not just one single high-speed highway, but refers to the national system of highways that connects the major cities and couples up with those of the neighboring countries. Think of the Autobahn as the German equivalent of the U.S.'s interstate system. The Autobahnen are as smooth as polished metal with no potholes, bumps, or uneven strips to interfere with the Germans' pursuit of driving

Beware of Blitzes

Germans' penchant for speed is kept in check by the presence of Blitz Cameras (called "blitz" because of the flash). These are metal-encased boxes that have radar and cameras inside and automatically snag speedy drivers. If you are unlucky enough to be "blitzed" then you can expect a speeding ticket in the mail a couple of days later. Being a tourist in a rental car doesn't exonerate you from the fine. Blitzes can be found anywhere from the Autobahn to a country road, and the kicker is that the authorities periodically move these around making it difficult to outsmart the Polizei.

Nirvana. No, these roads were designed for the hair-raising speeds for which Porsches, Benzes and BMWs are made to be driven. Germans build things to last and the Autobahn is constructed with a deeper gravel foundation and thicker pavement than American highways, producing a higher quality road and a veritable everyday racetrack.

Despite the widespread notion that the Autobahns are a free-for-all for speed demons, that is only partially correct. True, there are many sections of the Autobahn that do not have a posted speed limit (although there is a "suggested" limit of 130 km/h) and this is where you could easily find yourself doing 225 km/h or 150mph—if you had the proper automobile. More likely for the traveler, however, is that you will be traveling on sections of the highway that do in fact have limits ranging anywhere from 80-130 km/h—a far cry from the hair-on-fire speeds that have made the Autobahn infamous. Nonetheless, if you are like the average traveler to Germany, you will still get an adrenaline rush as you turn onto the highway and begin to accelerate to 110 mph, 120 mph, or higher speeds. You might be feeling pretty good as you top 125 mph: your Teutonic rental car is holding the road and has more horses left so you push it, hitting 140 mph and still going. No one is in front of you, you check your mirrors and no one is behind you either. You are cruising along, feeling damn good, if not just a tad nervous as you zip past blurred scenery. Suddenly, a 12-cylinder monster Mercedes comes out of nowhere and is bearing down on you, headlights flashing frantically and left blinker

Signage

While Germany has good signage that indicates the route that you are traveling, they typically do not reference direction in terms of North, South, East or West. Rather, direction is indicated by the cities and towns through which you may pass. For example: if you are traveling North on the A5 from Freiburg to Frankfurt am Main, you will need to know that you should pass Offenbach, Baden-Baden, Karlsruhe, Pforzheim, Heidelberg, Mannheim and Darmstadt before arriving at Frankfurt am Main (Frankfurt a.M. for short). While postings along the Autobahnen are generally clear, the situation becomes less obvious on the secondary and tertiary roads where the names of the towns are less familiar, so it behooves you to be sure of your route BEFORE you embark on your trip lest you end up in Frankfurt an der Oder on the Polish border, instead of at the international hub Frankfurt am Main. Germany's main highway system is the Autobahn, which is signified with the letter A (i.e. A2, A6, etc.), while smaller, but still main arterial ways, are signified with a B, for Bundesstrasse or State road. If possible, rent a car with navigation to avoid unnecessary "short-cuts".

on. You hastily move over to the right and let the Benz pass you as if you were standing still. What was just described is not an unusual scenario. When traveling the Autobahns at speed, you MUST always have your eyes forward, but constantly be aware of what is behind you at the same time because Germans drive fast and can be on your tail in no time. If you see a car approaching you from behind in the left lane with the left blinker on, that is not a driver who has simply forgotten to turn off the signal, it is a message. And that message is "move your ass over und schnell (fast)!" And if you are arrogant (or foolish) enough not to move over or simply oblivious, the driver will come within inches of your back bumper—and stay there—until you get the hint. So unless you have the mettle to drive at such speeds, the advice here is to get back to the right hand lanes. Still, for those of you fortunate enough to see Germany via its highways and byways, by all means give it a go. It's a great rush, but be mindful of your place on the road so that you may live to tell your story.

Traveling the rails in Deutschland is a treat and a somewhat less taxing mode than the high-speed affair on the Autobahn. Train travel in Germany is fast, clean, efficient, timely and safe—basically everything you'd want in a rail experience. There are train connections to nearly every town in the country that has more than 2 traffic lights and some to those with less. Because train travel in Germany is such a thing of efficient beauty, it is serious business. *Translation*: don't be late and understand and abide by the rules of the game. Trains arrive and leave the station at prescribed times and those times are adhered to stringently. While it is common sense that you should be on time to board the train, you should also be on time to *get off* the train. By that, it is meant that you will only have about 2-3 minutes to exit the train. If you are not near, or making your way, to the exit you may end up visiting the next town down the line because the conductors do not hold up the trains if you can't disembark. If you are one of those travelers who doesn't pack lightly, it may take you some time to get down the aisle and to the exit. Just as you are trying to exit, other passengers are trying to board with their own contingent of suitcases and bags. This, of course, leads to log jam in the narrow aisles and low and behold you are stuck—going nowhere except to the next station stop. In typical German fashion a high premium is placed upon punctuality and with literally thousands of connections needed to be made both domestically and internationally, Deutsche Bahn, the national rail company, does not deviate from the timeplan for any man, woman or child. In fact, in 1992, headline news was made when German rail made a highly unusual accommodation for a single mother with kids to delay their departure until her arrival. The exact details surrounding that are of less importance than the fact that efficiency and punctuality are paramount when traveling the rails in the Deutschland. During the high travel season, seat reservations are highly recommended. Should you be riding the rails during peak travel periods, it is not uncommon to have to step over sleeping travelers in the aisles because of overcrowding.

Germany's version of the bullet train, the ICE (Inter-City Express), whisks travelers throughout the country in comfort and style

Teutonphile's Tip: Train travel in Germany is a great way to see the country and lets you enjoy your trip without having to worry about a car. If you happen to be traveling in a group, the train can be extremely economical. On weekends, Deutsche Bahn offers up a "Schönes-Wochenende-Ticket" or beautiful weekend ticket. This ticket allows up to 5 passengers to travel together on the same ticket on any of the country's regional rail lines, all for around just Euro 30. For sure, the Bahn offers many other specials, but this one is great for those in a group looking to save some Euro. Check out www.bahn.de for more details.

Chapter 5

What's the Skinny?:
Nudity in Deutschland

The idea of being comfortable in one's skin is a relative concept. For some, it simply means to be comfortable with whom one is. The Germans, however, take it in a much more literal sense. For a people known more for being reserved and conservative, the Teutons do not appear to have any qualms whatsoever about stripping down—anytime, anywhere. Obviously, this is a clear exaggeration as you will not see the common German walking naked down the street, but what isn't an exaggeration is that the average German does not have any reservations about letting it all hang out. Beaches, lakes, mountainsides, camping sites, and, yes, even city parks are not safe from displays of immodesty.

While topless and au naturel sunbathing is the norm along the Mediterranean coast, you might be shocked to learn that all-nude sunbathing or *FKK* (which stands for *Freie Körper Kultur* and translates as the Free Body Culture), is also quite the norm in city parks across much of Germany. Interestingly enough, it was the Germans that pioneered the popularity of nude sun-bathing during the Roaring 20's, when Germany was a very progressive society—long before it came into vogue on the Riviera. Imagine this. After a few days of enjoying some of Germany's fine institutions of culture and heritage you decide to unwind for a few hours by exploring one of the many terrific city parks. No further than a hundred feet into the park you come across what looks like a nudist camp: people relaxing, eating, playing, and sunning themselves in the middle of the park—buck naked.

Flustered, you quickly pull out your trusty map, all the while keeping one eye trained on some of the more pleasant "sights", and check whether or not you have mistakenly veered off into some unknown forbidden zone. But no, your map has not steered you wrong, and you continue along the path, which winds through a mass of nudity. Now, we're not talking about a couple of dozen people here, but, literally, hundreds and sometimes thousands of sun worshippers making sure not to hide any body part from the sun's warm rays. Germans are so comfortable with the idea that they don't mind running around like the brunette beauty that I once saw bounding (yes, *bounding*) alongside a stream with her dog. Picture Bo Derek in the movie "10" running topless and you'll get the picture.

In some of Germany's larger parks, such as Munich's *Englischer Garten* (particularly around the ice-cold stream known as the Eisbach) and Berlin's Tierpark, there are vast swaths of land which are widely known by the city's inhabitants as FKK areas. No efforts are made to separate these sections from the other areas of the park; in fact, they may be the parks' biggest appeal! Try to envision strolling into New York City's Central Park or Boston's Common after

Nude etiquette

So what to do if you happen to be one of those more adventurous travelers who wants to get a little more of the, shall we say "German experience"? First off, let me remind you that while nudity is accepted throughout Germany, it is not condoned in all places, so don't pick the town's marketplace to "liberate" yourself. Second, try to select an area that is actually occupied by more FKKers than fewer. This way you won't "stand out" and it should ease any apprehension you may have. Third, don't sweat it! We all have one of two sets of equipment, so don't think that you will be the first naked person that your fellow nudists will have seen. Unless you are a knock-out model, don't be so vain as to think that everyone's eyes will be focused on you as you disrobe (there may be some eyes in your direction, but hey, what did you expect?) As for those of you who may be somewhat self-conscious about your own physical appearance, all I can say is that despite what the advertising world would have you believe, most people are of average physique (some better, some worse). Given some of the Germans that I have seen strutting their stuff au naturel, you'll have nothing to worry about. Some people bring blankets or towels to lay out on, others bring nothing at all, figuring that if they have their skin, they are adequately prepared. In general, gawking, staring and other obsessive types of behavior are not appreciated (although this is by no means a hard and fast rule—some may enjoy it). Although I have been witness to a couple of people who put on a little exhibitionist show, public displays of sexuality are generally an FKK no-no, so try to reserve any trysts for the privacy of your hotel room.

a day of sightseeing, only to see wide open stretches of grassy areas covered with naked skin! A fairly unlikely scenario for sure, but it paints a picture of what you may encounter exploring Germany's great city parks. In fact, many people flock to the parks, strip down and spend their lunch hour basking in the sun before having to finish out the day. During the summer in Munich, for example, the banks of the Isar river are teeming with nude sun-worshippers, regardless of whether it's a weekday or the weekend. Germany's cities are very livable places and the parks are a big reason for that as they allow its residents to literally shed away the encumbrances of city life and retreat to a more uninhibited lifestyle.

You will likely see couples taking in the sun's rays together, but you may be surprised to see groups of friends together drinking beer, playing Frisbee and otherwise just "hanging out". Or you may see entire families—mom, dad, sons and daughters spending the day like any other family, just doing it nude. Single men and women are also common. The "it's no big deal" attitude prevails at these locations and is approached with a banality that the idea of having clothes on suddenly seems inappropriate.

> **Teutonphile's Tip:** Get naked! For those of you who may not be entirely comfortable in your own skin, this would give you a great chance to shed some self-consciousness and follow the expression "when in Rome . . ." Moreover, your travel stories will be so much more interesting when you return home. Some recommendations for participating in FKK: the Englischer Garten in München, Tierpark in Berlin, banks of Lake Constance and the beaches along the Baltic coastline. University cities are more prone to nudity and as well as those in the south more so than in the north (simply a function of weather and climate), but on balance, should you have the urge to expose your posterior for the first time in your life, you will find ample opportunity in the BRD!

FKK is not only reserved for large city parks, but is just as likely to be encountered throughout the country. In small city and town parks, along the banks of rivers and streams and at the northern coast beaches, one can see "reserved" Germans basking in the sun. In fact, a beach on the Baltic coast in the town of Markgrafenheide is considered to be the biggest nude sunbathing beach in the world with over 10,000! nudists descending on the 15km (10 miles) beach during hot summer days. Markgrafenheide is about two hours north of Berlin in former East Germany. An interesting side note is that, despite the freedom to bare all, this beach is very restrictive with a lengthy list of *verboten* activities and items that are not allowed at the beach . . . go figure. As you might expect, the nudity quotient is higher in university towns, but by no means do nudists discriminate in Germany! There is no great political debate that

The Art of Relaxation: The Sauna

Many hotels throughout Germany have fitness areas which often include a sauna. Saunas in Germany are usually co-ed and they are also clothing-free, not clothing optional, but butt-naked. The whole point of the sauna is to sweat out the body's impurities and help with circulation; wearing clothing is contrary to that goal. Therefore, be forewarned that if you want to use the sauna you'll have to do it in your birthday suit. Also, when using the sauna you'll have to sit or lay on a towel so as not to get sweat on the wooden benches in the sauna.

occurs on this topic, no feminist uprising about baring one's breasts, or religious fanatics protesting such "sins". Rather, nudity is taken all in stride. FKK is not embraced by every German, mind you, but those that do, embrace it either partially or fully exposed. Otherwise, they don't worry about it.

Chapter 6

Wine, Women and Song:
It's Good to Be German

Unlike Germany's western neighbor, France, and southern friend, Italy, the Bundesrepublik does not enjoy either the wine culture or the international reputation for world class wines. Germany does not produce the sheer volume of wine that it's French and Italian friends can crank out, nor is it blessed with the more temperate climates critical for growing certain grape varieties. What it does have is very fertile soil, and temperate and arable hillsides along its many rivers that provide necessary cover and protection from frost as well as too much sunlight. Because most wine production is still concentrated along hillsides, harvest technology remains largely manual. As a result, the romantic images of tough-skinned workers in pointy hats, carrying long conical grape sacks, still can be had across most of Germany's wine growing regions. While I don't claim to be an oenologist, these factors help produce some of the most outstanding wines in the world.

In particular, German Rieslings are considered to be the standard-bearer for this light and fruity white wine worldwide. Germany produces nearly 40% of the world's supply, and the main growing regions for this style are in the southwest portion of the country along the Rhine, Main (pronounced *mine*), and Mosel river valleys, as well as many of their tributaries. Of less worldwide renown are red Spätburgunder (Pinot Noir) wines from Baden near Heidelberg and the Black Forest, as well as from the shores of the Bodensee (Lake Constance). Frankenwein, or Franconia wines, are concentrated around the city of Würzburg in northern Bavaria and are bolder and fuller-bodied whites than their

Riesling counterparts. These wines are lesser known because the growing regions are generally smaller, but also because the locals are very protective of their beloved wines and do not let too much of this quaffable treat escape local consumption. In many cases, certain styles of wine bottles are affiliated with the regional wines. For example, Baden wines often come in long slender blue or yellow bottles while Franken wines come in short, stout bottles, known as Bocksbeutel or literally "goat's sack" because it was originally stored in such sacks. Many of these wines are spectacular and no trip to Germany would be complete without trying some of the local wines.

Teutonphile's Tip: For something totally different check out Frankfurt's own version of wine, called Apfelwein or Apple wine. Known as Ebbelwoi (pronounced 'ebblevoy') in the local Frankfurt dialect, the drink is technically a wine, but is more akin to an alcoholic cider with a very bitter taste. The wine is served from gray salt-glazed pitchers with cobalt designs called Bembel into 1/3 liter glasses known as Gerippte. Apfelwein comes in four styles—Süsser, or sweet, is the mildest form coming directly from the presses while Rauscher, or smoker, is fermented longer and has one hell of a kick to it. Neuer Heller, or new wine, is served shortly after fermentation is fully complete while anything drunk later on is called Alter for older. With so many fine points it's easy to get caught up in the details. Although, personally, I can't stand the stuff (Stöffche), (which oddly enough is actually how most Frankfurters refer to Apfelwein), the best way to check it out is to get over to the Sachsenhausen section of Frankfurt. The streets of Neuer Wall and Textorstrasse are good bets for starters. Belly up to one of the long, crowded benches in the tight and often smoky Apfelwein taverns for a local taste. Several have gardens out back if you need to escape for some fresh air. To help you find establishments that serve up Apfelwein, look for a pine wreath outside. Since most Apfelwein is served in pitchers, you can impress the locals by ordering your Apfelwein using numbers. For example, if you are a foursome and each wants two glasses then order an Achter or 'Eighter.' One more thing, Ebbelwoi is best enjoyed with food since it can be a potent drink by itself.

A typical German wine label can be confusing, but provides a lot of information for making a good choice

Whether you make a point of visiting a vintner or happen to come across one in your travels, you'll be amply rewarded by pushing aside any hesitations and inquiring within. Many vintners have formal tasting rooms, while others offer you samples directly from the wooden vats, which are often stored in underground caves. A bottle or two of good German wine make great souvenirs or gifts and most vintners will happily ship a case or two home for you. Moreover, many vintners run Gasthäuser,

Inside the Wine: Knowing what's good and what's better.

As with most things in Germany, the labeling of wine is a regimented and regulated affair. With so many categories and sub-classifications, it's easy to get confused, and the German nomenclature is not for the faint of heart. Still, armed with just a little bit of knowledge, you'll be well on your way to making a great wine choice. In general the wines are classified by growing region and time of harvest. Below is a breakdown of the classifications to help you navigate your way not only in Germany, but at home as well.

Tafelwein—Table wine, or your basic jug wine

Landwein—Special table wine. A step up from the Tafelwein, this wine tends to have more character and body

Qualitätswein—Literally, "quality wine", or the highest general category of German wines. This category has two further qualifications:

Qualitätswein bistimmter Anbaugebiete (QbA) or "Quality wine of a certain growing region"—this classification tells you that the wine comes from one of the thirteen official wine-growing regions

Qualitätswein mit Prädikat—"Quality wine with a distinction" is the highest category of German wine and is denoted by one of six attributes which refer to the ripeness of the grapes in ascending order at harvest:

1. *Kabinett—Fully ripened*
2. *Spätlese—Late harvest*
3. *Auslese—Harvest of select, very ripe bunches*
4. *Beerenauslese (BA)—Harvest of individually-selected, overripe grapes. Tend to be very sweet and are primarily dessert wines*
5. *Eiswein—Ice wine, which are of the quality of BA wines, but are harvested and pressed while still frozen*
6. *Trockenbeerenauslese (TBA)—Harvest of hand-selected overripe and nearly dried up grapes. These wines are sweeter than BA or Eiswein and are rich and almost syrupy.*

or guesthouses, and you might end up overnighting in some idyllic little village while sharing dinner with the local family. With the proximity of many wine growing areas to Germany's rivers, river cruises are a great way to see the scenery, and place you directly in some of the best-known wine towns in Germany. While you can't go wrong with this option, try using the stops as jumping off points to further adventures just a few miles outside the main towns. You will likely have a more genuine experience and receive friendlier service. *Zum Wohl!* (Toast—"To your well-being!", i.e. health and happiness)

Although Germany is best known for its beer festivals like the über-party of *Oktoberfest* and, to a lesser degree, the *Canstatterfest* in Stuttgart (which 'quietly' attracts 4 million visitors per year—mostly German), wine festivals are far more prevalent. Most towns in and near the primary wine-growing regions hold some type of street wine festival. These are highly recommended since you get a chance to sample dozens of wines for nominal amounts of money and nearly all festivals sell you quaint one-tenth liter sampling glasses replete with town logo or some other symbol of import commemorating that festival. Here you can wander the marketplace or streets and contently down samples of local wines.

Chapter 7

Party Time:
Fetes, Fests and Fun

If you remain unconvinced that Germans are some of the biggest partiers around, even after considering Oktoberfest (although non-Bavarian, Germans will claim that Oktoberfest is not German, but Bavarian), then perhaps you need a little more evidence. Let's start with more modest levels of partying and work our way up to the big ones. Düsseldorf, the metropolis on the Rhein, where dark, malty Altbier flows freely, is home to the world's longest bar (*Längste Theke der Welt*). Technically not one continuous long bar, the *längste Theke* is so-named for the row upon row of taverns that stretch the lengths of the Flingerstrasse and Bolkerstrasse in this stylish city's *Altstadt (old city)*. Because patrons can sit and be served at high drinking tables that are permanently set up outside the roughly 275 taverns in this pedestrian area, it has the appearance of being one long bar when packed with beer-swilling patrons. Altbiers are served by waiters in proper white aprons, often two or more at a time because of the small 1/5 liter glasses and their immeasurable quaffability.

The Rheinlanders further to the south of Düsseldorf take advantage of the magical and mythical beauty of the Rhein's most storied stretch between Bonn and St. Goar. Beginning in May, and taking place at a different location five times during the summer, the Rhein is set on fire in what is known as *Rhein in Flammen* (Rhine in Flames). Rhein in Flammen is actually a series of fireworks extravaganzas that take place along the Rhein's most scenic locations and light up the night sky, as well as the surrounding vineyard covered hillsides and the ruins of castles where noblemen once ruled. So what does this have to do with partying? Well, for one thing, this section of the Rhein stretches along the highly-regarded wine-growing region that produces world-class Rieslings, so towns along the Rhein roll out the barrels of wine and put on special wine festivals for residents and visitors alike. Second, for each event, a flotilla of party cruise ships (usually 50-75 ships) disembarks and takes wine-swilling guests past the spectacular fireworks shows. The romance of the Rhein comes alive as fireworks rise above the mountains that line both sides of the river, illuminating the numerous forts, ruins and dramatic cliffs of the Rhein to create a stunning and exciting party-filled atmosphere. Both on the ships and along the banks of the Rhein, the spectacle is accompanied by classical and pop music.

*A flotilla of party boats cruise past the
Rhein in Flames extravaganza*

Teutonphile's Tip: With literally hundreds of thousands of spectators on the banks of the Rhein and 15,000 to 20,000 on board ships, each of the Rhein in Flammen extravaganzas is very popular and tickets for the ships are often sold out well in advance. Fortunately, there are 5 such events each year that you can take advantage of. The first of these takes place between Linz and Bonn, the second between Niederheimbach and Bingen / Rüdesheim, the third between Spay and Koblenz, the fourth between Loreley and Oberwesel and the final between St. Goar and St. Goarshausen. The shows last about an hour and reservations can be made for any number of ship companies. The best way of making a reservation is through one of the tourist offices anywhere along this stretch of the Rhein or in the bigger cities of Bonn, Köln, or Koblenz.

Back in the erstwhile and, once again, capital of Germany, Berlin, Berliners, Germans and other international visitors party it up along Berlin's main drag, Unter den Linden, at the Love Parade. Held annually in July, the Love Parade is befitting Berlin's status as a progressive, cosmopolitan capital city. Born in the age of techno music, raves, and the recreational drug, Ecstasy, the Love Parade has evolved into a weekend of peaceful debauchery, and all-day and all-night partying. Well over a million partiers crowd the boulevard to drink, party and love as passing floats blare techno music. World-renowned DJ's show up to spin tracks for the onlookers as they pass by on floats that double as their own mobile dance club. In what may be the modern day equivalent of Woodstock, revelers lose their inhibitions, their sobriety and often their clothes as they get high on the parade, the music and whatever else they may be using, despite an official no drug policy. Techno is big in Germany and the Love Parade celebrates it on a world stage and with flair. (Note: As Berlin has grown into its own since reunification, the Love Parade has been less welcome there and now has a new home in the Ruhr region's city of Essen.)

When one thinks of Carnival, the first images usually conjured up are of exotic, scantily-clad ladies, lively dancing and elegant floats parading through Rio de Janeiro, or even the mysterious masked and cloaked figures making their way through elegant Venice on their way to Carnival balls. In the United States, most think of New Orleans's Mardi Gras, but very few conjure up images of the crazy revelry that takes place in Germany and rings in the traditional, Lenten fasting season, but, in fact, that is exactly what happens. Largely a southern and Roman Catholic event, Karneval, as it's called in German, is an eruption of uninhibited partying and revelry along the Rhein and throughout southern Germany (although it continues to gain popularity in the predominantly Protestant northern half of the country). Like many Christmas traditions, Karneval has its origins in pagan rites and customs for expelling winter and welcoming spring, and all of the related imagery of blossoming, fertility and re-birth. Following the old adage of "if you can't beat them, join them", the Church, after a brief attempt to fight the long-standing popular traditions, decided to adapt the winter and pre-spring festivals to its own religious calendar. In the Rhineland, Karneval technically begins on November 11 of each year, but culminates in a crescendo of partying and craziness during the last week before Lent begins. Throughout the Karneval season, there are various costume balls, private parties, black tie affairs and booze fests, all known as *Sitzungen* (sessions), generally geared to raising money for floats and parades that take place during the week leading up to Ash Wednesday. Although similar, Karneval isn't the same everywhere. Germany really is a conglomeration of regions and Karneval typifies those provincial beginnings with its varying Karneval traditions and customs. Right off the bat, Karneval isn't even called Karneval everywhere it is celebrated. Cologne and the cities and towns of the middle Rhein, including Bonn and Düsseldorf, refer to it as Karneval, but just further south along the Rhein, the city of Mainz and its surrounding area call it *Fasnacht*, which literally means the "eve before fasting", referring to Ash Wednesday, or the last day before fasting begins. Still further to the south, in towns in the state of Baden-Württemberg, it is called *Fastnet* in the regional dialect. Bavaria and Austria use the term *Fasching*. In some cities, like Cologne, the climax of the foolish times is Rosenmontag, while for others it is what we know as Fat Tuesday or Fasnachtsdienstag. So now that we have gotten some of the cumbersome background out of the way, what really is Karneval in Germany? The highpoint of Karneval begins on the Thursday before and ends on the Tuesday before Ash Wednesday. These six days are considered the really *"tolle*

Tage" or crazy days. The essence of the *tolle Tage* is letting loose. Normally serious and reserved, Germans use this time to let their hair down and allow themselves a few days of uninhibited partying. It is an event so engrained in the local psyche that if you do not partake of the festivities, you are ridiculed and laughed at. The first prerequisite for taking part in Karneval is to don a costume. Costumes range from simple masks to elaborate costume ball wear, replete with masks, capes, and gowns. Elaborate make-up completes the look. Most common are the fools' costumes. Karneval has seemingly always been associated with fools, and the locals dress themselves in outlandish colors, crazy fools' hats, and generally outrageous garb usually meant to scare, shock or bring someone to laughter. Other costumes include clowns, various animals such as bears and boars, witches, devils, barbarians, and the like. Another favorite is to dress up like famous politicians as a way of mocking them. The most important thing in costuming oneself is to be somebody or something different. Local bars are so packed during Karneval that the partying spills out onto the streets as people sing, dance, drink and sway arm-in-arm. In addition to the costumes, the other ubiquitous thing about Karneval is noise. Incessant, clamoring noise coming from horns, drums, whistles and other noise-makers can be heard throughout the city at all hours during this time. It's the type of noise that is irritating and ear-piercing under most circumstances, but becomes music to the ears when you are drunk with merriment and enjoying the Karneval festivities. However, they don't sound so great if you are nursing a hang-over.

Karneval is such a zany and crazy time that the city of Köln actually selects a Carnival Prince known as '*Seine Tollität*' or literally 'His Craziness'. Here Karneval kicks off in earnest on the last Thursday before Lent, and is known as Weiberfasnacht or Women's Carnival. It is a day when women rule the men and evidence their freedom and rebelliousness by cutting off men's ties. Moreover, women are allowed to kiss any man they want to! Partying continues, more or less, unabated until Monday, when it reaches a feverish pitch. In Köln, this climax is reached during the Rosenmontag parade. Anywhere from 1 to 1.5 million people line the streets of Köln to watch and actively participate in the seemingly endless parade. Countless brass bands, costumed marchers and floats of all kinds depicting historical events, political satires and other, sometimes indecipherable, scenes make their way through the streets of Köln in this all day affair. Marchers and float participants throw chocolates, candies, flowers and other assorted items into the crowds who are singing age-old and newly-minted Karneval songs.

In Mainz, whose Karneval festival is second only to Köln's, its fevered partying culminates on the Tuesday before Ash Wednesday. Although second in size and popularity, Mainz's Karneval or Fasnacht festivities are televised throughout the country. In a marathon of performances, politicians are roasted, ridiculed and made fun of in witty satire. It's a bit difficult to grasp as an outsider, but the performances are humorous in their silliness, and it is fun to watch, nonetheless. Given its political slant, Mainz's parade includes costumers with oversized, distorted or caricatured heads of popular (and unpopular) politicos.

Although most of the serious partying and dressing up is left to the adults, children also participate in the Karneval activities. Certain days are designated as Kinderfasnacht and the kids dress up and come out to learn the Karneval ropes.

Ship of Fools

Entwined within Karneval, and inseparable from it, is the image of the *Narre* or Fool. Fools have come to represent all of the various forms of man's sins, and it is during Karneval that man acts upon those sins. It may simply come in the form of partying and general Tom-foolery. It may take the form of gorging feasts and, in some instances, it takes hold in adulterated activities. Karneval is a festive and open atmosphere, and food, drinks and kisses are all had in quantity and good-spirit.

Chapter 8

German Hip-Hop:
Klaus is in da Haus!

Ok, so you're saying to yourself 'German Hip-Hop', you've got to be kidding me!' In fact, that is exactly how I reacted to hearing about German rappers the first time. The concept appears totally incongruous with the guttural and perhaps harsh sounding language. In fact, that very same "harsh" sound makes the German language surprisingly well suited to rap (far more suited than, say,. French!). The German language itself has a tremendous number of words that rhyme and its cadence allows the singer to construct very rhythmic and flowing rhymes. In addition, the existence of various dialects accommodates the German rapper further.

So the Germans have hip-hop. Big deal, you say. Is it any good? Is it hokey? Does anyone actually listen to it? There are certainly more questions you could pose, but the answers to the above are, yes, maybe and yes. The first two are subjective, but the last is more fact than fiction. German rap does, indeed, have a popular following—probably not on a par with the following that rap enjoys in the U.S., but one that is growing dramatically. What is tremendously interesting is that while the origin of rap in the U.S. was a black/urban-driven phenomenon, a similar cultural scenario just doesn't exist in Germany. So, as much as it may be inconceivable that suburban, white kids in the U.S. have embraced a "gangsta" culture, there is no such equivalent in Germany, making the embracement of hip-hop even more surprising.

Given that music is subject to personal taste and preference, you'll have to form your own opinions of German rap music, but you should at least check out some local hot spots and music stores to sample the musical fare before dismissing German rap, out of hand. Some popular German rap groups are **Die Fantastischen Vier** (The Fantastic Four) and **Massive Töne**, to name but a couple.

In addition to the popularity of rap, Germany has a thriving music scene, ranging from rock and pop to jazz and classical. German hard rock includes worldwide icons, The Scorpions, as well as newer entrants, Ramstein, who have also had some success in the U.S. On the Pop/Rock scene, Germany has quite a few national stars with Herbert Grönemeyer coming to mind first among Germans, with his distinctive, yet soothing voice and his stand-out lyrics. Other popular bands worth a listen are German favorites, Pur and Blackföös. Given the language barrier, not too many German-speaking artists make it in the U.S., although there have been some notable exceptions, such as Nena and the late Falco of *Amadeus* and *Der Kommissar* fame (although he himself was Austrian). Moreover, *Volksmusik* remains popular in some areas, particularly in the south. While it's not for everyone, it seems perfectly suited for wandering the green foothills of the Bavarian Alps or the rolling hills of Schwabia. Germans have been on the forefront of the techno movement as well, and have been exporting their electronic sounds around the world to dance clubs and raves everywhere for years.

If you are a fan of 80's music, the Germans have a treat for you. In the early to mid 1980's, German bands churned out Pop-hits that were an eclectic cross between mild Punk and New Wave, and made up the style of music called *Neue Deutsche Welle (NDW) or 'New German Wave'*. In true 80's fashion, band members had big hair and wore lots of make-up. Songs consisted of happy, feel-good melodies accompanied by simple, catchy lyrics. Think back to when Volkswagen used the song "Da Da Da" in its commercials during the late 90's and you'll get exactly what Neue Deutsche Welle was all about. "Da Da Da", by the band Trio, was made famous in the U.S. by VW, but it was a hit way back in 1982 in Germany. This was not the first 'NDW' song to make it on the other side of the Atlantic. *99 Luftballoons,* by Nena, and *Major Tom,* by Peter Schilling, were other examples that made it in America, but there are dozens of hits known only to the Germans. Songs like *Eisbär* (Polar Bear) from Grauzone and *Hurra, Hurra, die Schule brennt* (Hurray, Hurray the School is Burning) by Extrarbeit were anthems to the legions of German kids who grew up during this time. New German Wave is experiencing somewhat of a nostalgic revival and you can find compilations of hits at any music store. If it turns out you like NDW then you might want to catch a performance by one of the NDW cover bands, such as Knutschfleck.

Whatever your musical preference, German music stores warrant a visit, and many have headphones for sampling the tunes. Buying some music is great way to get in touch with the culture and also makes for a great reminder of your trip. Even if you don't understand the words, check out some songs, as good music in one language tends to be good music in another.

Chapter 9

TV:
Late Night Comedy and Then Some

In Germany, late night TV is very popular, but instead of Letterman and Leno, Harald Schmidt rules the airwaves. "The Harald Schmidt Show" is modeled largely after the David Letterman show, but funnier. Tall, lanky with blonde hair and glasses, Schmidt is a nice German counterpart to Letterman. Schmidt has a musical companion as well, and the set is remarkably similar to Letterman's. Even if you don't speak German, you'll be able to grasp enough of the show to appreciate some of the humor. If you do happen to understand some German, sit down and enjoy an evening or two of Harold Schmidt—the comedy and the show are first rate. Speaking of comedy and humor, the German sense of humor is a little dryer than, say, Eddie Murphy's style, and is more like Jerry Seinfeld's. It is certainly more cerebral than British humor, as the Germans tend to favor witty over silly.

If comedy is not how you care to unwind, Germany offers you plenty of "spicier" options on regular television. Whereas eroticism and nudity are the domain of pay-per-view channels in the U.S., it is fairly prevalent on mainstream late night German TV. Anything from some *very* bad *Erotik* from the 1970s to contemporary adult-oriented films can be seen on channels such as Pro Sieben and SAT 1. In addition to films, late night TV has scores of commercials (sometimes 5-10 minutes at a time) with nude women (and occasionally, men) beckoning you to call for some naughty phone sex. Apparently the advertising barrage works, as Germans are Europe's biggest consumers of phone sex. Aside from the late night erotic adventures, prime time carries a number of sex-related shows, often providing "sexumentaries" on strip clubs, brothels, swing clubs, sexual activities and other sordid topics. Some favorite series include "Liebe Sünde" (Love Sins) which has had a multi-year run, reflecting the show's popularity. With such options, the late night viewer in Germany is never wanting for a little skin. Believe it or not, even the all sports channel, DSF, gets into the act by showing women working up a sweat in the nude, replete with grunts and moans. Imagine flipping through the channels to find the latest scores in the Bundesliga only to come across some lovelies working on their chest . . . muscles, that is. It's very surprising when you first see it, and a bit silly, but I wonder if ESPN would ever think about expanding its definition of sports?

Germans, in general, are news junkies. As the sidebar on radio highlights, news takes precedence over all else. It is not uncommon for Germans to read their daily newspaper, cover to cover and then supplement that with a weekly magazine. Their TV news fix comes in the form of Nachrichten TV or NTV for short. NTV is the German answer to CNN. German news tends to be more internationally focused, owing largely to its location in the middle of Europe.

Another peculiarity about German TV which you may encounter is what I'll call the "mountain channel". This channel shows real-time views of various mountain areas in the Black Forest, the Alps

Achtung, we interrupt this program to bring you . . .

Radio is radio is radio; but in Germany there are some peculiarities that you might find interesting. For starters, German music radio stations provide intermittent news updates about what's going on in the world. No big deal, you say. The difference with the German version of the news is that it is broadcast at the top and the bottom of the hour (i.e. 1:00 and 1:30 and so on). Again, that seems normal. What isn't so normal is that in the German world, news takes precedence over all else. So that if you are cruising along the Romantic Road, taking in the sights and be-bopping along to a song and the clock strikes one of those times, say good-bye to the song, because the news cuts in right over top of the song. Forget whether or not there were only 20 seconds left in the song or 2 minutes to go, the song is over and news takes center stage. While this is not a big deal in the grand scheme of life, I think it is another reflection of German order and punctuality. If the news is supposed to be on at the top and the bottom of the hours then, damn it, that is when it must come on. End of story, period. Forget about whether the audience cared to hear the end of a song, the news must go on.

and the Bavarian Forest, along with current weather conditions. The accompanying background music consists of traditional Volksmusik, yodeling and classic waltzes, all intended to lure you into dreams of hiking, skiing or just relaxing in Germany's mountain wonderlands.

Another peculiarity is that of the *Stau* reports. *Stau,* or traffic, reports supersede all else (although I can't tell you whether or not it would trump the news). If you are cruising along the A4 Autobahn between Freiburg and Frankfurt, for example, and there is a traffic alert, it will interrupt whatever you are listening to—and that includes a CD or audio cassette—in order to bring you the latest update on the traffic situation in your region. On the surface, it is a useful public service, but after a while I've found that it becomes an annoyance as every little accident has the potential to become an interruption. All in all, it's not too onerous but just another little reflection of German *Ordnung* (order).

Chapter 10

Oktoberfest:
The Mother of All Parties

With hundreds of festivals taking place across Germany, it's impossible to take them all in, but one festival stands out above all others, the world-renowned Oktoberfest. Sure, everybody knows that it's the biggest beer-swilling festival in the world. Some 6 million liters of beer are consumed during the roughly 14 day event that takes place annually, beginning on the third Saturday of September, and typically ending on the first Sunday in October. It originally took place entirely during the month of October, but for business reasons was moved up in the calendar to take advantage of better weather and warmer temperatures. What you might not know is that Oktoberfest is SO much more than beer drinking, although clearly that is the center of attention.

Origins of the Fest

Oktoberfest came about in 1810 as an event to celebrate the marriage of Bavaria's King Ludwig I to Princess Maria Theresa of Prussia. Historically speaking, this was significant in that it unified the southern Catholic kingdom of Bavaria and the northern Protestant kingdom of Prussia, forming at least the start of what is now modern day Germany. (Just as a side note, Germany didn't actually come into being as a country until the 1870's under the Prussian Monarch, Wilhelm Bismarck). Münchners organized 14 days of activities, including horse races, to celebrate the marriage. Because they had such a good time that first year, they decided to do it again the next year and have been celebrating ever since. In subsequent years, local merchants set up display booths to ply their wares, and the festival evolved, to some degree, into a merchants' fair. The big city breweries provided the libations, and the Fest has grown and evolved from a regional festival to a world-renowned event, attracting visitors from around the globe.

In addition to the beer drinking and camaraderie, Oktoberfest is a full-fledged quasi-amusement park. Not only are the fair-grounds filled with shooting galleries, games of chance, small merchant booths selling trinkets, cookies, candies and souvenirs, but it also has full-size roller coasters, a Ferris wheel, and other large-scale amusement rides, such as a parachute drop and the like. Lines for the rides move along efficiently in typical German fashion. Moreover, there are activities and smaller rides to keep children entertained. The pungent smells of roasted almonds, beer and smoked meat add to the atmosphere of merriment.

The modern-day Oktoberfest is a massive undertaking, which takes place every year at the Theresienwiese or Wies'n (pronounced Vee'zen) as the locals call it. The Theresienwiese was named in honor of Princess Theresa and is a fair grounds smack in the middle of Munich. Because of the throngs of people that invade Munich for this annual bacchanalian affair, the city decided to give the *Wies'n* its very own subway stop.

Contrary to what its name implies, that of a meadow, the *Wies'n* itself is mostly paved over. That being said, however, set in against the back hillside of the grounds stands the enormous statue of Bavaria, where she proudly reigns over the festival. (If you are so inclined, and sober, you can ascend to the top of Bavaria for a unique view of the Oktoberfest in all its glory). On the second Sunday of the festival, all of the bands from the various tents gather together alongside Bavaria, in their costumed garb, and put on a rousing performance that gets everyone in the beer drinking mood.

With six million people annually attending Oktoberfest, the Wies'n is a throbbing mass of people at nearly all hours. From 10:30 am to 11:30 pm, people gather together at long skinny tables that seat about 8 to a side (and sometimes more in a pinch) to drink and be merry. Therein lies the key and uniqueness of Oktoberfest. In the truest sense of the word, Oktoberfest is a *Volksfest* or "people's fest". Here, people from all over the world come together to enjoy some great beer and tremendous atmosphere, but above all, to get together with friends and strangers alike and share in the experience. Despite the hundreds of thousands of daily visitors, there are very few, scuffles; rarely do revelers succumb to that drunken syndrome known as beer muscles, because everyone is having too good a time to get worked up.

As far as some of the details go, let me give you a little better understanding of how things work. For starters, this whole idea of beer tents is greatly understated. These "tents", as they are referred to, are football field size pavilions with heavy load-bearing beams, wooden floors and walls. Some even have two levels and each comes with university-sized kitchen facilities and of course ample lavatory facilities. Each tent or Festzelt can officially accommodate from between 2,000 to 7,000 people inside (although those numbers swell on idyllic autumn weekends), and that doesn't include the hundreds of waitresses, cooks, attendants, security guards, and band members. To give you an idea of the enormity of the whole production, busy days can easily boast over 500,000 visitors. To most visitors, including yours truly, the sheer size and number of people may be the most astonishing part of Oktoberfest.

In total there are 14 tents, each affiliated with one of the city's old breweries. Construction of the tents begins well over a month in advance of the actual start of Oktoberfest. While each tent bears similarities to all the others in that they serve beer and have bands, each has its own personality. For example, the **Schottenhammel** tent, one of the smaller ones at the fest, is the territory of the younger and more beautiful set. It may be the least traditional in that the younger generations always add their own twist. In general, this tent has more locals than the others as Munich's youth gather here. Surprisingly enough, despite the younger generation's inclination to do things its own way, traditional Bavarian garb is all the rage here, and there appears to be a fashion contest of sorts. The **Hofbräu** tent, of Hofbräuhaus fame, is more of a tourist tent than the others, and also has one of the rowdier crowds. No surprise then that many Americans flock to this tent because of the name familiarity. I suggest that you steer clear of the Hofbräu tent because you will get a more genuine Oktoberfest experience at the others. The **Hacker** tent has, perhaps, the most scenic decorative motif. With its 'town square' backdrops framed by blue sky and clouds on the ceiling, you get the feeling that you are actually sitting outside enjoying the Bavarian sun, which is exactly what the brewer of Hacker-Pschorr beer wants, given its famous tagline of "Himmel der Bayern" or "Sky of Bavarians". The **Löwenbräu** tent is well-appointed in a blue and gold Lion theme, with the enormous Lion welcoming you into the tent. The most authentic experience is likely had at the **Augustinerbräu** tent, where you will find old men with real handlebar mustaches and wooden pipes, as if right out of 19th century Germany.

Regardless of which tent or tents you ultimately visit, you'll have a great time. That being said, seats in the tents are hard to come by and once you get one, stay there. Without a seat at a table, you will not be served. Because seats are at a premium, particularly on weekends, many locals reserve entire tables. Typically, tents mark off reserved and unreserved sections. Local businesses, many of which reserve the same tables year after year, take up the bulk of the reserved seats. As a result, the remaining seats are highly coveted, and people wander about trying to squeeze into a seat. While Münchners are usually cheery folks, they are not inclined to give up any reserved seats for visitors.

Because Oktoberfest is such an integral part of Munich life many local businesses keep shortened hours during the fest to allow their employees attend. Other firms shut down entirely for a day or two and the entire workforce goes to celebrate Oktoberfest together.

Although Munich is a cosmopolitan, international city, it still sits in the middle of staunchly Catholic Bavaria. In a rather unusual event on the first Thursday of Oktoberfest, a Catholic Mass service is performed in the **Hippodrom** tent for the owners, wait-staff and other workers at Oktoberfest; patrons can fulfill their religious obligations, atone for any sins of the past few days and drink with a clear conscience. Although this service is for Oktoberfest workers only, you can try to sneak a peek. If you do, you might even see babies being baptized. Imagine telling someone that you were baptized at Oktoberfest in a beer tent! And no, the beer is not holy water, although I'm sure at least one Bavarian may have suggested as much. In addition to offering Catholic Mass, the Hippodrom is renowned for its high numbers of celebrities who party—keep an eye out and you may see top models, soccer stars and TV and movie personalities.

Teutonphile's Tip: The Internet has leveled the playing field for visitors trying to get seats in the tents by letting users reserve seats on-line. Some, but not all, tents offer this option. Check out www.oktoberfest.de (it's in English and German) and click through the tent options to see which offer this service. While it's not critical to have a reservation, if you do go without one, be forewarned that on very crowded days, the tents fill up—often by noon and sometimes even earlier! Nobody can get in until somebody else leaves. The doors to the tents are shut and guarded by surly security officers. You may get inside after a few hours, but that is a long time to wait without a beer and I recommend getting there early, i.e. before midday, and on particularly beautiful autumn Saturdays and Sundays before 10:00 am!!.

Once you get a seat in one of the tents, you'll be greeted by one of the *very* hard-working waitresses, or *Kellnerin,* who will simply bring you a beer. Beers come in 1-liter glass mugs known as Masskrug and cost around 8 Euros. Cash is the best (and really only) method of payment and while tipping is not required, an extra Euro will ensure that you continue to be supplied with that wonderful liquid gold. With mugs that have wide tops, the beer goes down easily. Just to give you an idea of how much beer a liter is, it equates to about three (3) 12-ounce beers. So, even though it goes down smoothly and is helped along by the atmosphere of singing, dancing and swaying, keep in mind how much beer you may be consuming so that you are able come back for more merriment the next day. You may be surprised to learn that the beer tents also offer a full complement of food to go along with your beer. Pretzels and sausages are a given, but the kitchens have a full menu providing everything from soups to full plates of pork loin and sauerkraut. You certainly won't go hungry sitting there for 5 or 6 hours.

> **Teutonphile's Tip:** If I can offer one tip that you should heed regarding Oktoberfest, it is to be a consistent consumer of those tasty pretzels. Not only will they give you drinking staying power, they just might keep you from worshipping the porcelain god later that night (although they may not prevent you from having a headache the following day). One more thing: Germans don't eat pretzels with mustard so don't ask for any. Otherwise they will think you are certifiably nuts. If they do put anything on pretzels it is butter, but never at Oktoberfest!

With thousands of people drinking and being merry, the atmosphere in the tents is fun, but when you add in the oom-pah bands, that's when it really starts to get going. The bands play all of the traditional beer-drinking songs but I was stunned when I heard them break into renditions of John Denver's "Country Roads", the Beatles "Hey Jude" and the refrain from Bruce Channel's "Hey Baby", as well as other, more contemporary songs. The tents go nuts! As an American I find it totally bizarre and shocking that they absolutely love these songs and demand that they be played. Naturally, what's hot one year may not be the next. However the songs of the current year are so loved that you can walk through the streets of Munich during Oktoberfest and hear groups of people singing away as they return to their homes and hotels. Most amusing is to hear "Country Roads" sung by thousands with a German accent—now that's priceless amusement.

'Bavaria' proudly watches over the revelers at the Wies'n

If you keep your wits about you (which admittedly can be challenging in such an environment), you'll probably notice that after Germans, Italians—Italian men, to be precise—make up the next largest contingent of Oktoberfest merry-makers. In what appears to have become an annual guys weekend away, bands of Italian guys jump into tiny little campers and Winnebagos and flock to Munich for the weekend, leaving the ladies back in Bella Italia. As they descend upon the city, they park these little things anywhere that they can, and set up shop. Walking to the Wies'n on any given day, you are bound to see the Italians emerging from their cramped quarters to start the reveling. Toilets are at a premium, and showers are practically non-existent in these vans/campers, so you'll see them brushing their teeth on the sidewalk, sleeping in front seats, and cooking breakfast. After two or three days of this, these guys aren't pretty to look at, but they add a certain joi de vivre to the atmosphere. Still, should you come across some of these souls, take pity on them because they have to drive home the next day with major hang-overs.

Oktoberfest is also filled with its share of pageantry. The Opening Parade, on the first Sunday of the festival, shows off brewers and VIPs in ornate carriages and decorated horse-drawn beer wagons from the various brewers. Once the parade makes its way from the center of town to the fairgrounds, the city's Mayor taps the first keg and shouts in Bavarian dialect, "*O'zapft is!*" or "It's tapped!" to commence the annual revelry. If you don't want to fight for position among the crowd, you can get a prime spot for viewing by paying for tickets at the tourist office located at the main train station. Not to be missed is the procession of all of the oom-pah bands from all of the beer halls. Taking place on the second Sunday of the Fest, the bands all process down the main drag, past all of the beer halls and arrive at the Statue of Bavaria, where they line up on the steps leading up to Bavaria, and regale the crowd with booming beer-drinking tunes for a half-hour or so, before parading to their respective tents to kick off the partying. Back at the tents, the bands are greeted like conquering soldiers with raucous cheer and merriment, and the festivities then begin in earnest. The sights and sounds are a real treat, and this is a unique event to experience.

Oktoberfest really is the Mother of all Parties, making Mardi Gras look like a kindergarten party and easily surpassing the hoopla surrounding the Super Bowl. It is a party for Germans and foreigners alike and is enjoyed by people of all age groups. Grandmothers have no qualms whatsoever about standing up on the benches and swaying back in forth, arm in arm, with some teenagers in the tent. It truly is a Volksfest and should be a destination for anyone who can make it.

Chapter 11

Brothels, Hookers and Sex Shops:
Hanky Panky in the Vaterland

Well, sex pretty much happens in Germany the same way that it happens around the world, so you're probably not going to get any great insights into this topic during your stay, but there may be a few eye-openers for you. Despite what may be the general perception, Germans are a much more liberal and progressive bunch than usually thought, and this carries through on the sexual front. I'm not talking about perverse or deviant behaviors because, quite honestly, I can't speak to that topic.

Instead, there are some more general observations that can be made. For starters, public displays of affection are much more common and accepted throughout Germany than in the U.S. While teenagers the world over often fail to grasp the concept that "love is blind, but the neighbors aren't", displays of affection in public are fairly standard practice in Germany—on the subway, in a restaurant, at the train station; you name it, it happens. One time I was blown away when, in the middle of a crowded ferry boat on Lake Constance, a middle-aged man reached into his wife's blouse and just pulled out her breast and fondled it, right there in front of everybody! Another time, a couple on the subway in Cologne was getting so hot and heavy, I needed to move to another part of the car so that I didn't get caught up in the action. I can't even get into the time when a couple was putting on a show for all in the park to see. I'm not referring to outright public sex but more along the lines of . . . . well, keep your eyes open and you'll see for yourself.

Attitudes toward sex in Germany are somewhat confusing. On one hand, they are very open and liberal about nudity and the acceptability of premarital sex. On the other hand, many Germans, women in particular are reserved, while many men are "*kontakt-arm*" or lacking of human contact. This might explain the high use of phone sex, as well as a rapidly declining birth rate in the country, but that is pure speculation—some food for thought, nonetheless. Parents also seem to be more yielding to opposite sex friends spending the night in their teenager's bed.

Having discussed a little bit of background regarding German attitudes towards sex, it should help to explain attitudes towards prostitutes and the sex trade in general. Like every other country on the planet, Germany, too, has workers in the world's oldest profession. Unlike in the U.S., however, most prostitution in Germany is legalized. In fact, it's tightly regulated and controlled. While the concept of a red-light district is more of a metaphor in the United States, it is an actuality in Germany. Primped women sit in what are called *Schaufenster* or "show windows", which are illuminated with red lights, waiting to make a "sale" to their customers. In some of the larger cities, whole buildings are occupied by these ladies, and men can walk from floor to floor to pick out the perfect "companion". In most cities, such areas are located near train stations, where patrons can mix among the travelers and maintain some anonymity. In coastal cities such as Hamburg or Kiel, these areas are near the port.

In Frankfurt, which is the country's busiest transportation hub, the red-light district is a mere block away from the train station and the middle of downtown. Although Germany is not immune to occasional abuses, the prostitution industry is a highly regulated one, and the government even has its own inspectors. Women undergo regular exams, and condoms are required. In addition, inspectors have to check on the cleanliness and suitability of the rooms for the business to continue. As a rule of thumb, in case you decide to partake of such offerings during your trip, women who sit in the *Schaufenster* are legitimate and regulated, whereas those who walk the streets are not, and you may be exposing yourself to potential health or physical dangers. Every big city and nearly all small and medium-sized cities have their own red-light districts, so don't be surprised to come across such areas on your travels. Many are located around the train station, but others, such as the modest area in the sleepy city of Karlsruhe, are located in relatively quiet areas with pubs and residential housing. If you are traveling in mixed company, another rule of thumb to keep in mind is that men may look, but women should generally keep away. Photo taking is strictly forbidden, so don't even think about it, lest you find yourself being chased down the street by Hans (i.e. the heavy or the pimp), who may break more than just your camera.

Don't be surprised to see sex shops in respectable shopping areas, right next to the fashionable shoe store or clothing boutique. Sexuality in Germany is a much more open issue, which is why sex shops can be in primary shopping areas, and red-light districts are in very accessible locations. The ubiquitous **Beate Uhse** stores are the most well known, and are upscale and clean, so don't be shy. Less classy shops, as well as sex sideshows, can be found in the more seedy areas. Strip clubs are easy to find throughout the country, often right on the main streets.

> **Teutonphile's Tip:** A word to the wise: once inside these strip clubs—a common ploy that the "ladies" use to lighten your wallet is to ask you to buy a drink—one that may cost you upwards of € 50-75! What you may get in return for that drink is up to you, but just be aware that if you are just looking to drop a few Euros, you may be getting set up for a bigger score.

Chapter 12

The Sporting Life:
Fussball and More

In the world of sports, no sport is bigger or more popular than *Fussball*, or soccer. And in that world Germany ranks among the world's most important *Fussball* meccas. With three World Cup championships, five title game appearances and countless runs into the deeper rounds of the quadrennial tournament, Germany has made its mark on the world soccer scene. Add to that the numerous European Championships and you just might start to appreciate the importance of this game to Germany. For Germans, anything less than a championship is practically a failure, and the national mood can rise and fall with the fortunes of its soccer team. That being said, Germany's hosting of the 2006 World Cup, or *Weltmeisterschaft* (WM for short) was a watershed event for Fussball in Germany, and for Germany in general. The World Cup allowed Germany to showcase itself, its people, its culture, its progress since the dark days of WWII, its cities and towns and, perhaps, most importantly, its friendly and accommodating attitude. On top of that, the German team exceeded most expectations by reaching the semifinals, only to lose a heartbreaker against eventual champion, Italy. After being on the world's stage in the summer of 2006, Fussball-fever is at an all-time high and it may be difficult to envision any interest in other sports after its dream summer, but we'll get to that later.

Some fans take the saying 'become one with the ball', literally.

Germany has two top-level professional *Fussball* divisions known collectively as the *Bundesliga* or Federal Leagues. As you undoubtedly expected, the top professional level is the *Erste Bundesliga,* or First League, and then the *Zweite Bundesliga,* or Second League. This is where world famous stars such as Franz Beckenbauer, Matthias Lothar and Jürgen Klinsmann, among countless others displayed their athletic prowess before throngs of admiring fans.

Unlike the United States which has a number of big-time professional sports competing for the fan's attention, *Fussball* in Germany has nearly undivided attention. This creates tremendous notoriety for both the local city team as well as the national squad, which is cordially referred to as the *die National Elf,* or National Eleven.

With a dense population and relatively short distances between cities, local pride creates tremendous rivalries. Fans have an unmatched attachment to their teams, and the experience of sitting among thousands of swaying fans and listening to the many "fight" songs and chants can be sometimes surreal.

Although you can catch a soccer match practically anywhere you go, the German *Fussball* equivalent to the renown of the New York Yankees or Dallas Cowboys is Munich's First League team, **FC Bayern München**. The team's successful stature on the field is equaled by its home in the Olympic Stadium that was built for the 1972 Olympics. However, in conjunction with the 2006 World Cup, the team got a new stadium—a remarkable tire-shaped structure called Allianz Arena. If you are in Munich and can't see Bayern München, you can try to see the city's other, yet less successful, Second League team, **München 1860** (these guys are kind of like the Mets vis-à-vis the Yankees).

Munich's tire-shaped soccer stadium

In an interesting set-up, the top teams from the Second League can move up and replace the bottom First League teams, which then take their place in the Second League. This happens annually, and adds another dimension to the standings race. The musical chairs of leagues continues down the line. Teams that finish near the bottom of the Zweite Liga can get bumped out and replaced by teams from Germany's Regional Liga, which, in turn, can switch places with the Oberliga or Upper Leagues. In effect, the Regional and Ober leagues act like the minor leagues, something akin to Triple-A and Double-A in baseball. Depending upon when you visit, the teams in the various leagues may be different from year to year.

Teutonphile's Tip: Check out a game at any one of these cities that has a First or Second League team. Tickets will run you anywhere from € 5 to €50, depending upon team and seat location.

Erste Bundesliga	Zweite Bundesliga
Bayer 04 Leverkusen	Eintracht Braunschweig
Borussia Dortmund	FC Hansa Rostock
Borussia Mönchengladbach	FC Köln
DSC Arminia-Bielefeld	FC Augsburg
FC Bayern München	FC Erzgebirge Aue
FC Cottbus	FC Kaiserslautern
Eintracht Frankfurt	Karlsruher SC
FSV Mainz 05	Kickers Offenbach
FC Nürnberg	MSV Duisburg
Hamburger SV	SC Freiburg
Hannover 96	SC Paderborn
Hertha BSC Berlin	SpVgg Greuther Fürth
Schalke 04 (Gelsenkirchen)	SpVgg Unterhacking
SV Werder Bremen	Rot Weiss Essen
TSC Alemannia Aachen	SV Wacker Burghausen
VfB Stuttgart	Carl Zeiss Jena
VfL Bochum	TSV München 1860
VfL Wolfsburg	TuS Koblenz

(The abbreviations in the team names all reflect that it is some sort of club or association, i.e. FC = Fussball Club, SC=Sport Club, SV=Sportverein or Sport Association),

While soccer is the preeminent sport in the *Vaterland*, it is by no means the only sport followed. However, what passes for spectator sports is a little surprising. Germany has a growing professional ice hockey league, called the *Deutscher Eis Hockey Liga*, which has a league structure similar to soccer, with two levels of professional national play, and is quickly developing a professional basketball league (although a good portion of the players are Americans). More surprising, however, is the growing popularity of baseball. Amazingly enough, at a time when Major League Baseball is struggling to retain its fan base and keep America's youth interested in America's National Pastime, the popularity of baseball in Germany is booming. Baseball was first introduced into the *BRD* by the American armed forces stationed in Germany after WWII, but has really saw its interest grow during the 1990's as Germans' appetite for all things American grew. Presently there are nearly 30,000 Germans participating in organized baseball, according to the German Baseball Association, with some Germans having already broken into the Major Leagues. American-style football has also been a growing sport in Europe, but even more so in Germany. Of the six teams that comprise the NFL Europe, three of them are located in Germany: the Rhein Fire (Köln-Bonn region), the Frankfurt Galaxy, and the Berlin Thunder. As expected, given the sport's heritage as an American original, the NFL Europe consists largely of Americans. Most often, the NFL Europe is used as a proving ground for players who may need some more experience before moving up to the NFL, but as the NFL Europe gains exposure, more Europeans are starting to take the game up. That being said, don't hold your breath waiting to see an invasion of European football players onto the American scene.

While traditional American sports continue to gain in exposure and popularity in Germany, you are likely to come across more traditional hard-core sports like . . . Handball! Yep, Germany has a professional handball league with a full complement of playoffs and championship level play. If you happen to be channel surfing during your stay, you may have the fortune (or misfortune, depending on your viewpoint) of catching a game on DSF (Germany's answer to ESPN). Handball also gets frequent national and regional news coverage, which reflects the sport's popularity. In fact, in 2007, Germany hosted and won the World Cup of Handball.

Speaking of surfing, the folks in Munich have come up with a unique way to ride the waves without having the benefit of an ocean they have developed "river surfing". Some

Round and Round

Given their love of cycling in daily life, it isn't a stretch to think that Germans would be pretty enthusiastic about competitive cycling. There are hundreds of local cycling clubs and teams, but Germans also get into professional races. Not only are they serious about the riding, they are serious about the spectator side of it as well. Across the country there are dozens of cycling arenas (*Radstadion*), with some accommodating several thousand spectators. These arenas may be fully or partially enclosed, and are replete with restaurants for high class dining, full-fledged bars and the equivalent of luxury boxes for the well-healed and the corporate sponsor set.

creative Germans have adapted the great Hawaiian pastime of surfing using the resources available to them, namely a constant set of waves created by the Isar River. Forget about 30 foot swells in the Pacific. What we're talking about here is more along the lines of 1 to 1.5 meter continuous waves that are created as water flow passes over large rocks in the river bed. The surfers use boards that are more akin to oversized boogie-boards and jump onto them from the banks of the stream. When you first see it, it looks like something right out of a Hollywood film where the surfer is stationary and pretends to be surfing in front of some fixed background, but, in fact, these surfers are out there riding the waves like you wouldn't believe. Instead of riding a wave "in" to shore, these surfers ride the waves from side to side between the banks of the stream. Since the surfers don't actually have anywhere to surf to, the only way to (safely) end their ride is to simply bail-out with a back flop into the surf. While riding the Isar waves is technically not allowed, that doesn't prevent these surfers from taking to the waves and providing the rest of us with some free entertainment.

Surf's up in the English Gardens

Teutonphile's Tip: A great spot to see some local river-surfing is from one of the main entrances to Munich's Englischer Garten at Prinzregentenstrasse and Bruderstrasse. From the bridge over the Schwabinger Bach (stream) you have a bird's eye view to enjoy the entertainment and take photos.

Chapter 13

The Spa Life:
Soaking It All Up

Germany has a remarkably vibrant sauna and thermal bath culture, which reflects the country's obsession with feeling good and living well. Blessed with rejuvenating mineral water springs throughout much of the country, Germans have been enjoying the benefits of a good soak since the days when the Romans ruled the land. Throughout the ages, mineral baths have been sought out for their healing properties to cure or alleviate muscular and nervous system disorders, heart and circulation problems, skin ailments and a variety of other health related issues. The thermal bath experience has evolved over the years from the natural springs to soaking tubs to full-blown thermal bath complexes. In recent years, these bath and wellness complexes have sprung up all across Germany on a very grand scale, with some being able to accommodate several hundred, and even a thousand or so, visitors. Seemingly, every town that can claim some sort of natural spring is using that as its entrée into the spa industry. The German concept of a spa is a far cry from the watered-down American version. Whereas American spas revolve around massages, manicures and pedicures, facials and pampering, the spa culture in Germany is a much more elaborate, active and sophisticated affair.

The thermal bath offerings range from small hotels, with one or two whirlpools, to entire facilities devoted to health, wellness, relaxation and enjoyment. These larger *Therme* or thermal baths have several indoor and outdoor pools, soaking tubs, tubs with different mineral contents and different temperatures, and Roman-style bath houses with shallow soaking pools. In addition to the thermal baths, most of these spa centers have a variety of saunas. Some complexes have 20 or more different types of saunas ranging from traditional Finnish saunas to Russian Banjas to Turkish Hamams, where you lay on large flat stones, to various types of steam baths. These steam baths are often elaborately tiled in colorful Middle-Eastern styles, while many saunas are designed as replicas of old Nordic sauna houses. These complexes usually also have areas for getting a quick bite to eat or drink, and what would a spa in Germany be without a full-fledged bar to get a beer!

*Overview of the enormous thermal bath
and spa complex Therme Erding*

After any amount of traveling in Germany you should treat yourself to one of its many thermal bath and sauna complexes to unwind, relax and recover. It not only will reinvigorate you, but it will also give you a great opportunity to mingle with the locals, and the beauty of it all is that a day at the baths is very affordable—a typical 4-5 hour stay costs only about €20-30, depending upon whether you opt for the sauna facilities, which are €5-10 extra.

If you do take advantage of one of Germany's best leisure activities, there are a few things you should know that will ease your initiation into the thermal bath and sauna culture. First of all, because you are not likely to be traveling with your own bath towels, you should rent them at the cashier's counter for a modest fee. Two are recommended, particularly if you intend to use the saunas. Also, if you so choose, you can have use of a bathrobe, although it is not necessary. Once you pay at the counter, you will receive a wristband that includes a key for a numbered locker and a "chip". This chip, which is on the wristband, is your all-access pass. It gets you through the turnstiles, keeps track of your time, tallies any food and beverage purchases and allows you to purchase any additional services such as massage or tanning salon time. At most places, the sauna section is separate from the thermal bath section, so if you initially purchase admission only to the baths, your chip will get you into the saunas and you will make up the difference upon your exit. Once you have your wristband, proceed through the turnstiles to enter the changing areas. You first encounter changing rooms (*Kabinen* for cabins) that have doors on two sides. Enter through the one side, change and exit the other side where you can find you numbered locker and store your things. The locker rooms are unisex and not separated for men and women. If you are using the thermal baths, bathing suits are required; however, if you are using the sauna facilities, these are *textilfrei* or no clothing areas. While this can be disconcerting at first, you shouldn't let the liberal attitude surrounding nudity at the spa prevent you from experiencing a great sweat. The no-clothing policy is two-fold in nature. First, it is designed to keep the facilities clean and minimize germs and, second, it doesn't interfere with the whole purpose of the sauna, which is, after all, a good *Schwitz*—and clothing only gets in the way. Once you've changed and made your way to the actual facilities, you can chart your own course as to how to plan your stay. While many sauna fans adhere to a strict regimen that includes a pattern of sauna followed by cool-down and relaxation, it's entirely up to you how to spend your time. You can spend your time sweating away in the saunas, soaking in the minerals in the baths, getting a good steam in the *Dampfbad*, or, if you just want to relax and enjoy, you can use the indoor or outdoor pools and hot tubs or stake out a lounger in the aromatherapy or quiet room for a quick nap. The scope and variety of options at these complexes is shocking and, at some of the bigger ones, you probably could not experience all of the variety in a single day. For many Germans, a day at the baths is a great family outing. The kids can play in the pools and take advantage of the waterslides and splash parks, while the parents relax in the various wellness areas. Since you can spend many hours at the thermal baths, the facilities have cafes and bars that serve everything from pork cutlets and sausages to snacks, and from fruit smoothies and coffee to beer and wine for your eating and drinking needs.

Take a trip back to ancient Rome in the
soaking bath at Therme Erding

The Germans are so into their spas that they devote lots of time and energy to creating unique spa experiences. Many spas open up the entire complex on Friday and Saturday evenings and other special occasions, both the thermal bath side and the designated sauna side, for FKK or no-clothing nights. Others put on elaborate Pink Floyed-esque light shows, both in the water and on the domes of the facilities. Still others have theme nights, such as Karneval, and many host special holiday parties for their guests. It's quite an undertaking, and the largest of the thermal bath operators are now even selling the equivalent of private spa "condos" at their facilities so that frequent customers can have privileged access to the best services during their relaxation time.

A day at the thermal baths can be a great way to experience the best of Germany. While the saunas tend to be quiet (often required) so that people can fully relax and enjoy a good sweat, the pools and whirlpools tend to be more convivial, with more splashing around and friendly conversation. Some of the larger facilities have retractable domes that cover the entire facility. During the summer months and on nice spring and fall days, the roof is retracted, which gives the experience an island resort feel. Contributing to this feeling are the palm trees, and sandy beach areas that some spas have.

Holy Water

The spa and mineral bath culture is deeply ingrained in the German psyche and even though much of this could be credited to the Romans, none other than Charlemagne did more for its popularity. Charlemagne, better known as Karl the Great (Karl der Grosse) in German, conquered much of what is western Europe in the 8th century A.D., and unified Europe as much as anyone could ever say Europe is unified. After being crowned Emperor by the Pope, Karl the Great set up shop to govern his Holy Roman Empire in the northwestern city of Aachen. The selection of Aachen on the Rhein was no accident. Emperor Karl, a lover of swimming and the invigorating and healing powers of thermal mineral waters, chose Aachen because it, allegedly, has the hottest natural thermal springs north of the Alps. There are numerous spas throughout Aachen, and you can even take a drink of the sulfur-rich waters at one of Aachen's public thermal fountains.

Teutonphile's Tip: Many spas have package deals with local hotels and/or the regional transit authorities. These can be very economical ways to get discounted entrance to the spa and transportation, particularly if the spa is located outside of the major cites, which many are. Inquire at your hotel or ask at the town's tourist office for discount information.

If you'd like to learn more about the various spas throughout Germany there are several websites, including www.insauna.com as well as travel guides that give details for specific spas. However, most spa guides are in German only and may require more than just a rudimentary knowledge of the language.

Chapter 14

Bicycling:
Life on Two Wheels

While bicycles are ubiquitous in China, a rapidly growing country of over a billion, you might be surprised to learn that Germany, a country of a mere 82 million is probably more bike crazy than China. In contrast to America, where bicycling is seen more as a leisure and recreational activity, bicycling in the *Bundesrepublik* is an integral part of daily life.

Although Germany has one of the most efficient and densely integrated systems of public transportation in the world, it is the bicycle that is often the preferred method for getting around. The traveler to Germany should not be surprised to see doctors and executives commuting to work via bicycle, even though buses, trolleys and trains are readily available. Mothers take care of the daily errand runs by bike, and their bikes can be seen laden with groceries and other goods. Sometimes children too young to ride their own bike are carted around in their own two-wheeled carriage, almost like a motorcycle side-car, but attached at back. Most of the big cities and many smaller towns have a full complement of designated bike lanes. We're not talking about just a couple of bike lanes along the main thoroughfares, but an entire system of bike lanes that criss-cross the city along with roads and sidewalks. Right of direction and way are clearly marked and cyclists have their very own signage as well as automated traffic signals that ensure efficient crossing at busy intersections. As with most things in Germany, bicycling is serious business, and riders are required to properly maintain their bikes. If not, the police can—and do, issue citations and fines for broken headlights and the sort. All bicycles are required to have a front and rear lighting system, as well as a bell to let other riders and pedestrians know that you are around. Even though you may think that a bell on a bicycle is only for 6 year-old girls, if you hear one in Germany, be careful to make sure that you are not in a cyclist's path. If you find yourself walking aimlessly along the sidewalk, taking in some of the splendid sights, be sure to keep in the *Fussgänger* (pedestrian) path, otherwise you may end up being on the wrong side of a tongue lashing for being a *Dummkopf*. Since Germany is a fairly structured society, which, in many ways, is why it works so well, Germans are not shy about policing themselves. So, if you do happen to be reprimanded, don't think that your hosts are being unfriendly—they're simply keeping it real (and orderly).

A streetlight for cyclists—cyclists have to follow rules, too

Cycling in Germany works so well because population densities are fairly high in towns and cities. Despite having a population of 82 million living in an area only about the size of Montana, roughly two-thirds of the country remains undeveloped (either farmland or forests and natural habitat). From a practical standpoint, that makes the bicycle a necessity, but Germans are a health conscious bunch, (yes, traditional German meals may suggest otherwise) and they view daily cycling as part of their natural fitness regimen, even if not in the usual "work-out" sense.

While cycling seems to be natural in the warmer months of the year, Germany can be a cold and wet place during the winter, and one would expect that the bicycle is put into hibernation for the winter months. Not the case however. If you happen to be in Germany during the cold months, don't be surprised to see countless cyclists riding throughout the cities in downpours, snow or sub-freezing temperatures. The Germans have a saying about cycling and inclement weather, which pretty much sums up their affinity for cycling: "There is no such thing as bad weather for bike riding, only bad clothing". Although snow sometimes puts a dent in the number of riders, Germans are out there in every type of weather. When there were times that I wanted to ride the trolley or catch a bus, my German compatriots insisted on *Radfahren* (bike riding) despite what I considered arctic-like conditions.

Seeing Germany like a German—

If you're interested in seeing the country in a unique way, try a bike vacation. For all but the most avid and well-equipped cyclists, the best way to do so is to book a trip with a travel agent. Most trips are set up so that you bike your way from town to town, and a service forwards your bags to the hotel at the next town. These types of trips are usually quasi group affairs. You bike at your own pace, but you are generally, among a group of people following the same itinerary. Because most of the people taking these types of trips are Germans, this is a casual, relaxed way to meet everyday Germans and get to know them. Many of the best trips are structured so that the route utilizes the country's trains and river boats to get you to the most scenic stretches. With so many sights to see and bike trails to choose from, you probably can't go wrong with your selection, but there are some particularly recommended routes. Some favorites include scenic rides along the north shore of the Bodensee (Lake Constance) from Meersburg to Friedrichshafen. Along with picturesque villages, this route offers spectacular views of the lake and the Alps to the south. Vineyards abound on the north side of the lake, and stopping in for a tasting or lunch at one of the many vineyards is a relaxing treat. A ride along the grand Rhein between Koblenz and Cologne offers up many medieval villages, ruins of castles and more wineries!. You can cruise through the rolling hills of the sleepy, but beautiful Lahn river

Because biking is such an integral part of daily life in *Deutschland*, many companies provide separate (and usually more favorably located) parking areas for cyclists. If you should happen by one of Germany's fine universities, expect to see, literally, hundreds of bicycles lined up outside the classrooms. Other indications of the seriousness of cycling are the occasional protests declaring *"Radwege statt Autobahnen"* (bike paths instead of roads) or the fact that the train system, the *Deutsche Bahn*, permits bicycles on most trains for just a modest fare increase. Many trains headed to vacation destinations in the warmer months have cars outfitted specifically for bicycles.

valley, starting from the old university city of Marburg through Limburg of Limburger cheese fame, and on to Koblenz. This is an area not known very well to tourists, and represents a nice off-the-beaten track itinerary. Depending upon your stamina, skill level and preference, you can take a long easy cruise on any number of routes in the flat north, such as along the Elbe River near Hamburg, or a challenging ride through the mountains of the enchanting Schwarzwald (Black Forest). There is no lack of opportunity for cycling in Germany, so get a move on and hop a bike for the day or more, and explore Germany the way the Germans do!

Cylcing is not just for practical purposes. Germans are avid cyclists and there are thousands of established routes. Most bookstores in the Vaterland have an extensive section of bike maps that can provide you with possible trips. With so many to choose from you are often faced with *Die Qual der Wahl* or, roughly translated, as the "agony of choice".

Given the extent of bike paths and cycling in Germany, you should take an opportunity during your trip to rent a bicycle and cruise around the city. It's the best way to see many of Germany's treasures, and allows you to get in amongst the *Volk*. You'll see some great things that you may otherwise miss on a bus tour, and be able to cover much more territory in shorter periods of time than by walking. Bicycles work particularly well in Germany's medium and large cities where sights and attractions are spread out. They are especially well suited for cities such as Berlin, Munich, Cologne and Hamburg that have relatively large, flat land areas, making the pedaling easy on the legs. If you are just renting a bike for a day or two, your best bet is to rent from nearly any of the country's train stations and rates are reasonable at just $10-15/day. They are centrally located, making pick-up and drop-off a cinch and for more avid cyclists, or those planning on spending several days in one locale, it may make sense for you to check out one of the handful of local bike shops, which provide rentals. While daily rental rates are generally reasonable, be prepared to put down a deposit of Euro 50-100—a credit card works best. Before pushing off, make sure that your bike is in proper working order and importantly, make sure that it comes with a functioning lock!

Chapter 15

Food in the Fatherland:
Beyond the Wurst

German food is more than just sausages and potatoes, although they do occupy a high rung on the German food chain. Still, German food or *Essen*, doesn't get the respect it deserves. Everyone knows and loves Italian food with its rich marinara sauces, hearty pasta dishes and succulent fish while culinary snobs everywhere point to French cuisine as the pinnacle of taste bud delight. German food, however, with its reputation for hearty meat and potato dishes, commands little of the same respect. That perception, while having some truth to it, sells the German food story a little too short. Contemporary German food is more varied than it was fifty, or even ten, years ago, and is influenced by many regional and international tastes.

Certainly, we associate schnitzel and sauerbraten with Germany, but how about *Maultaschen*—meat and spinach-filled ravioli, (known as or "mouth pockets") or various forms of potato casserole. Frankfurters and Bratwurst are surely German, but what about the dozens of other kind of Wurst or sausages, such as Bierwurst, Thüringer and Nürnberger or even *Weisswurst*. Because these are more complex sausages to produce, we often don't see them in our home country, but they are everywhere in Germany. *Wurst* is not just served with sauerkraut, Germans also have *Wurstsalat* or sausage salad. In its translated form, it doesn't sound so appealing, but it is a tasty green salad that is not really a sausage salad at all. Rather, it is topped with strips of light cold cuts.

Soups abound, ranging from asparagus soup to cheese and potato soup, as well as very brothy, boullion soup. Butchers (look for signs for *Metzgerei*) regularly carry venison, duck and even hare for variety, while open-air markets for fresh fruit and vegetables are found in every city and town. Fondness for all things fresh means that the average German still ventures to town markets on Saturday mornings to pick up the weekly supply of Obst and Gemüse (fruits and vegetables). Despite the loosening of shopping hour restrictions, most Germans, particularly *Hausfrauen* (housewives), are still programmed to do their shopping on Saturday mornings, when you'll find shopping districts and markets busiest. If you are on a tight budget, or just want to grab some fresh fruit for the road, these markets are your best bet for getting the best stuff for your travels. An effort at speaking a little German might also yield an additional plum or two.

Perhaps surprisingly, Germans are large consumers of vegetables of all types, reflecting a healthy eating orientation. Chicken and turkey, as well as ham and beef products, are regular items on the German table, while pasta dishes, such as *Spätzle* and spaghetti, are common as well. Often, *Spätzle* is served with marinara sauce instead of the traditional butter and cheese topping. The aforementioned foods are very much the common thought when German food comes to mind. What doesn't come to mind are the seafood dishes prepared with fish from the North and Baltic Seas, as well as Lake Constance (*Bodensee*). *Matjesfilet* or herring fillets are very popular. Nor do people consider the regional specialties that are often influenced by the neighboring countries. For example, in the southwest, where Germany shares a border with the erstwhile French province of Alsace, or *Elsass* in German, *Zwiebelkuchen* or "onion cake" is a popular dish. Resembling a pizza, *Zwiebelkuchen* has a dough base to which onions are added. Various spices and options, such as meats,

Phallic Obsessions

Despite being a meat and potatoes kind of Volk, the Germans do have one curious love affair with a vegetable. That vegetable of choice is *Spargel*, or asparagus. The German version tends to be whiter, and have a bit more girth to it, than our slimmed-down, green version. Spargel season runs from the middle of April until the end of June, and the Germans go crazy over it. There are Spargelfests, Spargel contests and, in some places, they even crown a Spargelkönigin, or Asparagus Queen, complete with tiara. Spargel is usually served with a Hollandaise cream sauce, but during Spargel season, you can get Spargel soup, Spargelpizza, Spargel casserole and, yes, even Spargel cake. Spargel is usually a fairly bland vegetable, but for some reason, Germans have a passion for this phallic vegey and, with their usual enthusiasm, Germans have raised a common vegetable to superstar status.

cheeses and vegetables can be added as "toppings", and the *Kuchen* is baked to make the dough crispy. Add a little salt and voilá, you have a light, yet tasty little meal. In some instances, a touch of alcohol is added, and the *Zweibelkuchen* is ignited and served as *Flammkuchen,* or "flaming cake". Given the large numbers of foreigners in Germany, particularly Turkish, quick meals of lamb meat, either in a Gyro form or Kebab, can be had in nearly every town.

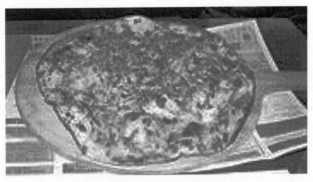

A typical Flammkuchen

Teutonphile's Tip: Steer clear of "American style" bars and fast food restaurants. If you're on an extended stay of 30 days or more, and cruising the continent, it's all right to treat yourself to a little familiarity since Germany has its fair share of fast food joints like McDonald's, Pizza Hut and KFC, but if your stay is of shorter duration, try local restaurants and Imbissstube (deli-like joints). You'll get more authentic meals and a better value for your Euro, as well as sampling some of the local faire. Imbissstube and other quick eateries serve up hearty portions of chicken and fries, kebabs, cucumber salads and sausages, cheaply. Many are now run by foreigners, so you can also find Gyros, Doeners and Currywurst for a little variety. Besides, when your friends at home ask you what exotic foods you tried, you don't want to have to respond with a "Royale Deluxe with Cheese" (aka McDonald's Quarter-Pounder with Cheese). Also, don't be afraid to enter any of the butcher shops, where you'll also be able to order a ready-to-eat fresh sandwich, or Leberkäse.

Although French bread may get more play in Hollywood movies, it is the Germans who are really the bread connoisseurs. Germans consume bread with practically every meal: *Frühstuck, Mittagsessen and Abendessen*. In fact, Germans even use the word *Abendbrot,* or evening bread, to refer to dinner in many households! Germans have a much greater variety of breads than their European neighbors do. You've got wheat breads, black breads, rye breads, mixed nut breads and farmers' breads, to name just a few. Germans almost have an addiction to bread, and without their daily fix of the doughy stuff, all is not right with the world. They are so obsessed with bread that there is actually a Bread *Museum*. The *Deutsches Brotmuseum* is located in the city of Ulm in southern Germany, and could be a quick stop off, if you are there visiting the world's tallest church.

Although traditional German food is still rooted in meat and potato products, German cuisine is much more varied today, with influences from across Europe as well as Asia and America. Not all dishes have rich, heavy sauces, although many do; but many have light sauces or generous use of spices. As Germany has become more international, its food has started to reflect that, as well, with items like Hawaiian pizza, Middle Eastern delights and Asian delicacies showing up on menus around the country. Be sure to try some unusual dishes if you have the chance, but if you happen to be like me, and thoroughly enjoy traditional German food, go with what you like, but don't sell German cuisine short. *Mahlzeit* and *Guten Appetit!*

Chapter 16

Politics, Politics:
The German Version

One of the first things a traveler may come to realize, when encountering Germans, is that conversations quickly, and almost undoubtedly, turn to the topic of politics. Conversations in cafes, bars, beer halls and, even around the family table, often focus on the political theme of the day. Whether it is a discussion of regional political elections or international diplomacy, you will find that Germans are quite knowledgeable on many fronts. Not only are they knowledgeable, but opinionated too—sometimes a little too opinionated in the author's experience. In one instance, a young man proceeded to tell me what the U.S. was all about and how we should fix our problems—and he'd never even been to America! Talk about your audacity. In other cases, I have met Germans who seemed to know more about American politics than most Americans, and they naturally felt compelled to provide unsolicited suggestions as to how we may "improve".

Whereas Americans may shun political discussion amongst friends and family as too sensitive to introduce while sipping coffee or beer, Germans relish such talk. Why all the interest in politics? Well, for starters, Germany is a very educated and literate society (95% literacy rate) where it is not uncommon to see 30-year-old students at the universities (personally, I think this has to do more with the carefree lifestyle that they lead rather than with education, but *So ist das Leben*—so that's life). However, with all of this education comes a culture that is aware of local, national and international affairs and has a great interest in debating the merits of current *Politik* (policy).

Germans have other reasons for being inclined to discuss politics, too. Most importantly, is the fact that the country is situated smack in the middle of Europe. It shares a border with nine different countries and acts as the western gateway to emerging Eastern Europe. Moreover, modern day Germany is a work-in-progess, and trying to fuse together a country from the democratic West and one from the communist East has produced some unique challenges. So purely from a practical standpoint, it behooves Germans to be well aware of, and vocal, about the policies and politics of the day, since they, more than in any other country in Europe, are affected by the policies enacted within and outside its borders.

With nine friendly neighbors and strong ties to the United States, international politics would likely dominate any political discussion you may have with Germans. If you happen to be one of the nearly 2 million Americans who travel annually to Germany, you can most definitely expect to be in the hot seat regarding any political discussion. As a citizen of the world's only superpower, you will be the subject of much debate. If you are up on current political topics and are so inclined to debate these points with your newfound friends, it can be a very enjoyable and interesting experience, albeit, at times, potentially frustrating. Either way, you represent your country, and the Germans will give you ample chance to espouse your views, but will also take twice as much time to espouse theirs!

Since economics follows politics, the German appetite for political discussion is also driven by its importance as an economic power. The BRD is Europe's biggest economy and the third largest in the world, behind only those of the United States and Japan, and is largely an export driven economy. Automobiles, chemicals and machinery are among the country's biggest industries. Because of its relative importance within Europe as well as the world, economic policy-making is critical and, hence, the subject of much political debate. As a traveler engaging in an economic-political debate, you should be aware that while Germany is a free-market society it has some important differences with the Anglo-Saxon model of capitalism. For starters, German corporations have responsibilities to more than just shareholders; corporations are required by law to consider the welfare of their workforce and the communities in which they operate before undertaking major decisions. Profit is still the major driving force for German companies, but this is often balanced against the greater good of the community it serves, thus giving Germany its label as a social marketplace (*Sozialmarkt*).

While political discussions are often fodder for pub and café chatter, by no means is politics the only topic *des Tages (of the day)*. Don't be surprised if one day you are sitting at a table with Germans, in a Biergarten, and one of them suddenly launches into a diatribe on the Chancellor's latest social program or the European Union's foreign policy (or lack thereof). If you should get engaged in such a conversation, take the opportunity and fire back; jump in feet first and don't worry about offending Germans, because they are

> ### *Debunking the myth of German conservatism*
>
> In American political terms, the concept of left and right, or liberal and conservative, is largely equated with Democrat and Republican. While Germany is a democracy, and shares many of the same values as other western democracies (no surprise since the US and its western allies provided the political framework for modern Germany after WWII), do NOT assume that the German notion of left and right or liberal and conservative parallels that of the United States. If one were to compare Germany's political spectrum with that of the United States along the lines of Liberal, Moderate and Conservative, Germany's spectrum would line up wide left, meaning that what the average Germany considers conservative is what the average American might consider liberal. Of course, in making such a statement, there is naturally room for a wide range of interpretation on this topic. Nonetheless, the point is that Germans are a liberal-leaning society in American terms. A number of European countries would also likely fall into such a description, so it's all relative. Without digressing into the nitty-gritty details of the differences between U.S. and German policies, Germans are much more opposed to capital punishment and gun ownership, more tolerant of alternative lifestyles, including same-sex marriages, adoptions, and spousal benefits, stricter as it relates to environmental issues and maintain more of a pro-labor stance than in the United States. While the list could continue, it is important to be aware of these differences, but, at the same time, keep in mind that the value system is still fairly comparable and is separated by a matter of degrees, not magnitudes, of powers.

very difficult to insult. Germans are straightforward and direct, and as such, appear to have developed a thick skin through the ages. So, if you're trying to insult them, just be prepared for a lengthy process. It's a great chance for you to learn about views and opinions on the other side of the Atlantic and you might just make a couple of friends in the process, even if you ultimately decide to disagree. However, after 3 or 4 of some of Deutschland's finest beers, you all tend to agree anyway!

Teutonphile Tip: Achtung! One VERY important distinction that any traveler to Germany should understand is that while the Republican party in the United States is an established, legitimate political party, the Republican party, or Republikanner, in Germany is considered by most to be a right-wing extremist party with ties to the neo-Nazi movement. While any German recognizes the obvious distinction between the two parties, despite the commonality of the name, you should be sure not to lump the American Republicans in with the German ones, lest you find yourself in the uncomfortable position of being verbally accosted! Conversely, don't let the Germans lump the American Republicans in with the German ones either!

Chapter 17

Bier hier!:
A Beer for All Seasons

Germans have a well-known international reputation for their love of beer, but in actuality, it goes beyond just tasty enjoyment. Beer, as a topic and a drink, occupies an important role in the German psyche. So important, in fact, that some common phrases include references to beer, such as *"Das ist doch nicht dein Bier!"*—literally translated as "That is certainly not your beer!" but means "That's none of your business!" Then there are the Bavarians, who elevate their love of beer to an entirely different level. For them, beer is considered a basic food, and that is not just lip service. Members of the German Army, who are stationed in Bavaria, are allotted a one-liter daily ration of beer because the Bavarians consider beer to be a staple of their diet, just like bread and meat.

Unlike many other developed countries, where the beer industry is largely controlled by just a handful of relatively large players, Germany's beer industry has been more resistant to consolidation. For starters, beer is very much a local product, with a local, or at least regional, brewer supplying the large majority of beer to that area. Secondly, Germans are sticklers for their beer quality, with brewers adhering to the German Purity Law of 1516 or *"das Reinheitsgebot"*, which states that beer shall only be comprised of four natural ingredients: water, malt, yeast and hops. In recent years, this has created some controversy within the European Union, as the Union's rules are less strict than are those in Germany. Nonetheless, the existence of this rule, and the strong local affiliation to a particular brewer, has kept the industry fragmented. The good news for us is that Germany has an amazing number of beers to offer its citizens, which are of the highest quality and have relatively low prices (a glass of beer is cheaper than a glass of soda, for instance).

*Different beer styles demand different glasses
for full enjoyment*

Unlike taverns in the U.S., pubs in Germany are supplied by just one or two brewers, almost always including the local one. As such, if you find yourself sitting in a pub or restaurant at the foothills of the Alps, you may only see offerings from **Löwenbräu** or **Erdinger,** for example. While this is fairly standard practice throughout Germany, you should be aware that there are several common styles found throughout the country, including *Pils* or pilsner beer, which is a clear, light and usually somewhat bitter-tasting beer due to its high hop content, *Helles* beer, a clear lager, as well as *Export* beer.

A beer by any other name

Across Germany, but particularly in the southern portion, wheat beers are very popular. So popular in fact, that Germans try to confuse the unknowing by giving this beer several different names, hoping to frustrate them into ordering something else, thus keeping even more of this refreshing style to themselves! Despite the cryptic nature of the nomenclature, they all essentially mean the same thing. As such, a standard wheat beer will be known as both a *Weizen,* meaning wheat, or *Weissbier/Weisse,*

Seasonal brews make appearances throughout the country as well; springtime harkens brewers to put out a strong *Maibock* beer, while, in the fall, the all-important Oktoberfest beers make their presence known, and winter gives rise to various Christmas beers and dark bock beers. Given the varied regions in Germany, many regions, or even cities, have their own style of beer.

In northern Bavaria, *Rauchbier*, or smoked beers, are common, and are the result of smoking the malts before the brewing begins. In the Rheinland, several local styles can be found, from *Köln's* famous light and fruity *Kölsch* beer to the strong, dark and sweet flavor of Düsseldorf's *Altbier*, or literally, "old beer". *Altbier* is so named by virtue of the fact that it is brewed according to the "old" method, which means that it is a top-fermented ale, as opposed to the "new" method of lager-brewing, which developed in Europe after ales. Dortmund, in the industrialized Ruhr region, also has its own style called *Dortmunder Export*—a golden lager, which is a heartier version of a Pilsner. In Berlin, the Berliners enjoy their own tart version of wheat beers with shots of berry flavored syrups that give the beer a red, green or even blue color, depending on what flavor you choose. In the south, wheat beers (see sidebar) are a staple, even used to wash down the morning helping of *Weisswurst*. With the thousands of breweries that still exist in Germany today, no single discussion of beers could exhaust the numerous styles and variations that are produced throughout the country. Still, whether you are a connoisseur or just a casual

meaning white, for its lighter color. In addition, unfiltered wheat beers, where secondary fermentation takes place in the bottle are alternately known as *Hefe-Weiss* meaning yeast-white beer or *Hefe-Weizen*, meaning yeast-wheat beer. Whatever the name the local brewer uses, the beer styl is the same. You most certainly will also encounter dark versions of these same wheat beers, preceded by the word *Dunkel*, or dark. Most wheat beers are unfiltered, giving the beer its hazy appearance, but when the yeast and sediment found in traditional wheat beers is filtered out, the beer is then call a Kristall Weizen for crystal or clear wheat beer. Despite all of the machinations surrounding the naming of wheat beers, be assured that you will be getting wheat beer even if it is by some other name. A similar scenario also befalls the amber Oktoberfest beer style. This beer style is interchangeably referred to as a Märzen, or March beer, because, before the days of refrigeration, the beer was brewed in March, then stored or lagered in cool beer cellars and caves through the summer, only to be brought out in time for the harvest and fall festival of Oktoberfest.

appreciator of beers, you should seek out and sample a variety of what Germany has to offer.

Teutonphile's Tip: Despite the purity requirement for brewers stipulated by the Reinheitsgebot, that hasn't stopped German beer drinkers from experimenting and mixing their own beer concoctions from the finished product. You might like to try a Diesel beer, which is a mixture of Pils and cola, or a Radler, a summertime favorite that is a mixture of beer and lemonade (or Sprite). Sounds odd, doesn't it? If you are a beer purist, and like your beer to taste like beer, you might not find these chemistry experiments so tasty. But, if you are willing to open your taste buds to some unusual flavors, both of these options may surprise you, and you can easily take the idea back home.

Just as the brewing of beer is serious business, so is the actual drinking of it. To Germans, a proper pour is almost as important as the beer itself. No self-respecting Deutscher would accept a beer without about an inch of smooth, foamy head on it. A substantial head is an indication of proper carbonation and also releases some of the aromatic flavors of the beer. Although no hard and fast rule exists, a proper pour of a Pils should take about seven minutes, meaning that you may need to exercise some patience after ordering. What may be perceived as slow service could, in fact, be just an adherence to good beer pouring etiquette. Speaking of etiquette, whenever Germans are drinking among others, they make a toast in almost ritual-like fashion. It usually begins with raising the glass, clinking the glass and uttering a phrase such as *Zum Wohl*, or *Prost*. This is followed by a light, quick tap of the bottom of the glass on the table and then, finally, lifting the glass to your (by now) parched lips, all the while keeping eye contact with your drinking friend(s). Although not adhered to by all Germans, if you follow this pattern you will quickly be in the good graces of your German drinking friends.

Chapter 18

Working at Germany, Inc.:
You Call That Stress?!

After World War II, Germany orchestrated what is commonly referred to as the *Wirtschaftswunder,* or economic miracle. Totally rebuilding its cities and towns, industries and transportation networks gave rise to Germany's reputation as a hard-working and industrious nation. Without disparaging those from the former East German state, the German Democratic Republic or DDR, here I am referring to the former West Germany, although much can be said of the DDR as the standout economy behind the Iron Curtain. For sure, Germany's reputation is deserving in many ways, as the country has an enviable infrastructure, boasting first-rate rail and highway networks as well as other modern utility systems.

But while Germany, as a country, has many accomplishments to name, individually, Germans aren't the sort of folks to forego a little rest and relaxation—quite the contrary. The average German worker receives six weeks of vacation—standard! That's right, six full weeks, or 30 days, and that doesn't include an allotment of sick days as well as national, and often times, regional holidays. Add it all up and your average Deutscher is off about 8 weeks or, essentially, 2 months out of the year! I may simply be jealous, but if you are only working 10 months out of the year and getting paid for 12 months, I'm not sure how this hard-working reputation is justified. I'd like to write it off by saying that Germans work more hours per day than the rest of us, but that sure isn't the case either. The average workweek in Germany is approximately 35 hours, as companies reduced work hours to spread the pay around, in order to keep more people employed (the folly of this scheme is fairly self-evident). So, how in the world can Germany stay competitive with Americans, Japanese and Brits, who on average receive closer to 2-3 weeks of vacation per year? Essentially, as it stands now, it can't, and Corporate Germany is having to swallow some bitter pills and make some big changes to keep its competitive standards up. But that will be a challenge as well. Why? Because Germany has legislated it that once a person gets a job, it is nearly impossible to fire that person. Oh, you thought that that whole thing about reducing work hours and spreading the pay around is done out of the goodness of these companies' hearts? Come on now, profit still remains the biggest motive, so don't think that companies are happy about this situation. It's simply a function of very powerful unions and the country's community mindset, which, in and of itself, isn't necessarily a bad thing. As an employer, if you happen to hire a less efficient worker in the Vaterland and want to replace him or her, forget about it, because you are plain out of luck! Talk about job security, it's practically job guarantee. As an employee, it is certainly nice to have such protection, but it comes at a great cost to entrepreneurship, innovation and future growth, as inflexibility hinders advancement. As

***Need a day off?* . . .**
Just blame it on the Föhn

If you happen to be in Southern Germany, particularly in and around Munich, but also along the Bodensee, you may hear about an interesting weather phenomenon known as the Föhn (pronounced, Fehrn). The Föhn is a wind that flows rapidly down from the Alps. The wind itself generally originates in the Sahara desert and blows north across the Mediterranean and over the Alps. As it rises up the Alps, the air loses its moisture, and cools in the decreased pressure at the high altitude. Once it comes over the Alps and begins to descend, the air is compressed, and the result is a dry, warm, strong wind. The wind can clear a cloudy sky and raise the temperature 20-30 degrees, leaving you with an idyllic day, replete with blue sky and warm breeze—even in the middle of winter. While this may be a traveler's dream, it tends to wreak havoc among southern Germans. For reasons not entirely clear to the scientific community, the Föhn tends to make people irritable and cranky. Incidents of headaches, sleepiness and even nausea have been known to be higher when there is a Föhn wind blowing. Greater numbers of accidents and arguments also occur, and students get restless. While the Föhn wind is not entirely unique to southern Germany, it does appear to affect Germans more, resulting in increased absences from work when the Föhn gusts. So, if you don't feel like working or going to school on an unusually warm, clear day—just blame it on the Föhn!

I've mentioned in the introduction, Germany is a country steeped in tradition, and right now it is attempting to adapt to a rapidly changing world, so it should be quite interesting to see how things shake out.

Despite all the time off, the short work week and the job security (not to mention the rather generous benefits), you will still hear our Teutonic friends griping about how *ausgestresst,* or stressed-out, they are. Everyone, of course, has his or her own perception of stress, and it's no different in Germany than anywhere else in the industrialized world, but the Teutonic version appears somewhat watered-down. I would gladly make a "stress" trade with my German compatriots.

With so much time off, how *do* they afford all of their vacations? Well, first of all, Germany is a wealthy nation, so that helps, but there is another, dirty little secret about the over-worked, stressed-out Deutscher. On top of the six weeks standard vacation time, many employees receive vacation money. This is not paid vacation, but rather is additional money paid to the worker in order to actually go on vacation. Vacation money varies by employer and contract, but can range from 1-2 weeks. Not a bad deal, if you can get it. Let's do the math here: if we add in the relatively standard 1 month's bonus pay (*Weihnachtsgeld* or Christmas bonus) that the average worker gets, he gets 13 and one-half months pay for 10 months of work. Sign me up!

As you can see, it's rough sledding in the BRD and, as you can imagine, it's a tough gig trying to figure out how to spend six weeks of vacation per year, but amazingly, they accomplish this, although it's probably with a little bit of stress too.

Chapter 19

European Delivery:
Car Buying the German Way

Germans have done a good job over the years of exporting their love of cars. While the automobile in America is the ultimate symbol of independence and freedom; for Germans it is a symbol of technological and engineering prowess. Nowhere is this mentality more evident than in the high-quality cars that roll off the assembly lines at BMW, Mercedes-Benz and Audi, not to mention the hot rods from Porsche (that's "poor-sha", not "poorsh"). Cars produced by these manufacturers are designed to be driven at the high speeds that are both legally permitted on and mechanically suited for the Autobahn. Germany possesses the densest network of roads in Europe and, despite their love of trains and efficient public transportation, Germans also covet their autos. The good thing for us is that they've also made their love of driving the Autobahn accessible for us, if not necessarily affordable. Introduced in the 1970s as a way to endear Americans to the brand, BMW started its European Delivery service for Americans, whereby Americans can place an order for a new BMW at a dealer in the United States and pick up the car in BMW's headquarters city, Munich. Since then, Mercedes-Benz and Porsche have followed suit and offer similar pick-up programs, both handled out of Stuttgart.

If you are considering buying a new BMW or MB, European Delivery is the way to go. Let me outline the process as conducted by BMW, the leader in this area.

The first thing you need to do is place an order with your local U.S. BMW dealer. The advantages of buying a car this way are several-fold.

First is price. Because you are technically taking ownership of the car in Germany, the car is not subject to various import/export taxes, and the base price of the car is about 7-9% less than you'd pay in the U.S. Depending on the model and price of the car, this can save you anywhere from $2,500 to $5,000 off the U.S. price. Because you will be purchasing a build-to-order car, you are advised to place your order 90 days in advance of the day you want to pick the car up to ensure your travel and pick-up plans match the factory production schedule. Given this amount of discount, the European Delivery option effectively pays for your trip or at least defrays some of the cost of the trip. Keep in mind that you then also do not have to rent a car, which can easily cost in the hundreds of dollars, particularly if you want to rent a high-end German make. All of the paperwork is handled by your U.S. dealer, and he works with the manufacturer's European Delivery department to ensure that your car is built as ordered and on schedule for the designated delivery date. Because you are taking ownership of the car in Germany, all of the financing needs to be completed at least 2 weeks in advance of your travel date. In addition, there is some minor incremental paperwork, such as passport and driver's license information that needs to be completed so that your new car can be properly registered and insured in Germany. BMW offers 14 days of free insurance and up to 90 days can be obtained at reasonable prices through BMW's insurer. Lastly, you must submit a copy of your valid passport to your dealer. Once the dealer has your payment and paperwork all that is left to do is fly to Munich and pick up your car. In advance of your departure, BMW will send you a nice package of information that includes visitation tips for Munich, such as walking tour maps, subway maps and other local information. Additionally, they provide you with specific details as to how to get to the delivery center.

Once you get to Munich, you can either take a taxi to the delivery center or use the efficient subway system which has a stop just steps away from the center (take the U3 to Olympiapark). The delivery center is actually part of BMW's sparkling new BMW Welt (World) complex, which has exhibits, restaurants and shops all intended to showcase the BMW brand. Once inside, make your way to the Premium Lounge and all you need to do to get the process started is give the representative your passport and the wheels will be set in motion. Although processing time at the delivery center can vary, most deliveries take about an hour. Since it takes about 20-30 minutes to get your paperwork in order, you will be escorted to the café where you can get a quick bite to eat, tea, coffee and, of course, beer. Leave it to the Germans to give customers beer before they pick up their snazzy new cars to drive on unfamiliar roads at high speeds. As part of your pre-departure materials, BMW of America provides you with a voucher, so anything you get at the café is on them. While your anticipation level rises, you can try to relax with a newspaper or magazine, but, shortly, your name will be announced and someone will sit down with you to go over the formalities surrounding the registration, insurance and paperwork on how to return the car for shipping back to the U.S. It's all pretty academic stuff, and you'll then be escorted to your sharp new car, fully detailed and ready to be driven. The representative will go over all of the features of the car with you in English, and you're out the door in 20-30 minutes.

It is a professional and efficient process, and you'll be on your way in no time. As far as returning your car so that it can be shipped back to the U.S., BMW, along with Mercedes has a number of locations in key European cities such as Vienna, Zurich, Rome, Paris, Stuttgart and Frankfurt, where you can drop off the car. Simply call ahead to one of these locations and let them know when you will be doing so. The drop-off procedure consists of filling out a few forms and leaving the keys. The rest will be taken care of for you.

A tourist license plate

Teutonphile's Tip: if you want to keep the German tourist license plate that is on your car, have the folks at the drop-off location remove it for you, and take it with you in your luggage, because it won't come across the ocean with your car. Also, cars in Germany are required to have a safety triangle and a basic first aid kit, which don't come with U.S. delivered cars, so if you want those items as well you'll have to take them with you.

Many people who take delivery of their cars in Germany take advantage of the factory tours to see where their cars were "born". It is a nice complement to the entire experience, and details can be obtained from the manufacturer.

Chapter 20

The Sky's the Limit:
Peaks, Skyrides and Zeppelins

Sometimes the best way to see a country is from the top, and the Germans seem obsessed with climbing or somehow getting to the top of every peak, look-out point, church tower, hill, mountain top, or any other man-made or natural structure that gives them a chance to stare in wonder and say, "*Ach, wie schön!*" or simply, "wow, how beautiful!" You know, in a lot of ways they've got the right idea. Taking in a city, town or landscape from above does give you a great appreciation for the beauty of the place, and making the trek to the top of anything always brings with it some level of satisfaction that you've made it.

There's nothing like climbing up a 100 meter, steep, crowded, several hundred year-old church steeple to cure your fear of heights and claustrophobia, all at the same time. But that is exactly what may happen if you climb to the top of the some of the highest church towers in the world, including the world's highest. There are thousands of church towers that you could climb throughout Germany, and should you encounter some that strike your fancy, you think a climb to the top would enhance your trip, by all means, get going. But there are a few towers that are absolute musts in Germany. The first is the Cathedral of Cologne (*Kölner Dom*). Perched upon the banks of the Rhein River, this imposing structure with its dual spires can be seen for miles when approaching the city. Despite the severe damage it sustained during WWII, the Dom served as a symbol of inspiration for returning residents after it was assumed that the church was completely destroyed during

Allied bombing raids. Today the church stands proudly, housing its unique treasure—the bones of the Three Wise Men. Despite such treasures, the real gem is the climb up the 509 steps to the top of the tower, where you can enjoy a commanding view of the city and the Rhein valley that stretches for miles up and down the Rhine and into the mountains of the neighboring Red Hair range to the east. At 157 meters, the tower of the Kölner Dom is high, but it is not the highest in Germany. That honor goes to the city of Ulm, where its *Münster* rises nearly 162 meters and seems to touch the heavens. In fact, the Cathedral of Ulm's church tower is the highest in the world, and it is not uncommon for the weather at the top of the steeple to be different than that on the ground. While not having the benefit of a large city like Cologne to look down upon from the top, the Münster does provide unequaled views of the Alps to the south on clear days. While you have to pay a modest fee for the privilege of climbing 768 excruciating steps, it's well worth it, and you'll be just like a true German if you do.

Just 768 narrow, circular steps separate you from the top of the world's tallest church in Ulm

There are a few other noteworthy towers that are musts if you visit these cities. The TV tower in former East Berlin's Alexanderplatz affords you a view of this expansive city and the surrounding area, and you can see how the Spree River snakes its way into, through and out of the city. Germany's signature skyline city, Frankfurt, has numerous viewing options, with the architectural jewel, the *Messeturm* providing unrivaled views of the Frankfurt skyline.

But the best views of Germany come from much higher up. Although Germany possesses only a sliver of the Alps, what a sliver it is. Because it is at the northernmost edge of the Alps, Germany's highest peak, the *Zugspitze*, provides the equivalent of a wide-angle lens shot of the east-west situated Alps. At 2963 meters, not only can you see Switzerland and Austria from this peak, but it is rumored that on the clearest of days, you can see all the way into northern Italy—probably a little white lie, but telling, nonetheless. In addition, because the mountain itself straddles the Austrian-German border, you can even cross over into Austria at the top. Before the days of unchecked border crossings in the European Union, this was a bigger deal, but it is still rather unique.

The Zugspitze is the pinnacle of the German world

In the heart of the Black Forest (Schwarzwald) sits the charming city of Freiburg, and the best way to see this city and get a good look at the *Schwarzwald* is to go to the top of the 1284 meter high *Schauinsland* (literally, "look into the country"). Despite their affinity for climbing, the ever-industrious Germans have built small-gauge railroads and cable-cars to get you to the tops of these mountains. To reach the Zugspitze you have to take a combination of railway and cable car, while the Schauinsland can be reached by cable car. Perhaps the wildest view of all comes from the cabin of a Zeppelin. Completely taken out of service in 1940, just three years after the Hindenburg disaster, Zeppelins have been flying the southern skies of Germany since 2000. For the best views of the Alps and Germany's largest lake, the *Bodensee*, or Lake Constance, take a ride on the new and improved Zeppelin airships of today. The Zeppelins take off from Friedrichshafen (where there is also a Zeppelin museum) and float around the Bodensee, offering breathtaking views of the Alps and green-blue waters of the lake.

Teutonphile's Tip: The modern day airships are a far cry from the days of the Hindenburg. Kept aloft by safe helium and using an internal frame, flights on the Zeppelin are subjected to the rigors of modern aviation safety measures, so that shouldn't stop you from taking a ride. What might stop you, however, is the steep price tag. A one hour trip can cost nearly €300,-per person! But if you can afford it, it is an experience to remember. Contact the Deutsche Zeppelin Reederei at www.zeppelinflug.de or the Tourist office in Friedrichshafen at www.friedrichshafen.de.

Chapter 21

Floating Away:
Life on the Water

Despite their penchant for speed, the Germans do, in fact, allow themselves a little leeway for leisurely trips. Most notably this occurs on water, when they are not necessarily as concerned with getting from Point A to Point B as fast as possible, although punctuality is still prized. Some of the best means for seeing the sights are on boats, and certain cities in particular are well suited to these often-overlooked boat tours. Boat trips are ideal ways to see cities and towns in ways not readily available from land. In the North, with its greater numbers of waterways, you can catch tour boats in the cities of Hamburg and Bremen for great views of the cities. You'll get to see the big ports up close and see how these cities developed and continue to thrive. Some of these tour boat captains seem like cowboys zipping in between large cargo ships and in and out of the various canals in the old warehouse districts. Less hair-raising is a boat tour around the old, port city of Lübeck, which was once a trading powerhouse and part of the Baltic Sea Hanseatic Society. Near Berlin, small flatboats take leisure seekers on peaceful trips down the Spree River, through the quiet *Spreewald* or Spree forest. A trip through the Spreewald is like being transported back in time a hundred years. Old forest villages still adhere to age-old traditions and flatboats still act as a primary means of transportation between some of these outposts. Pleasure cruises can be had on the Rhein and Danube rivers, where boats shuttle people up and down the river to enjoy the centuries-old ruins of castles, quaint riverside towns and the old churches and abbeys where spirits and bitters are still distilled. Although not to be missed, the scenic trips along the Rhein can be packed with tourists. For something a bit more "German", try a cruise along the *Donau* or Danube. The Danube starts high in the mountains of the Black Forest, but the river doesn't become passable until near Regensburg in Bavaria. Either in Regensburg or Passau, you can board a boat which will take you through the heart of lower Bavaria for a unique view of Europe's longest river. But, perhaps the best example of Germans taking it easy on the waters is in Bavaria. In true Bavarian revelry, in spring and summer, groups of Germans board enormous 20 meter long and 8 meter wide wooden rafts and float down the green-blue waters of the Isar River, from Wolfratshausen to Munich on what is known as a *Flossfahrt* or log-raft trip. Professional oarsmen guide rafts, and rafters are accompanied by a Bavarian band and treated to snacks of Bratwurst, Leberkäse, and pretzels, not to mention copious amounts of beer. Rafts are constructed of huge tree timbers and sport wooden seats, serving booths in some cases and, yes, even stylized Port-A-Potties for the roughly six hour and twenty-five km float. During the trip, up to 55 partygoers drink, sing and be merry, all the while passing idyllic Bavarian villages, and even careen down a log flume. You may even come across some of those ubiquitous nudists along the banks of the Isar River. *Flossfahrt*s also take place on the Danube or *Donau* as well. Places on the rafts are tough to come by as many firms reserve entire rafts for company outings. Still, if you are interested, the best way to reserve a spot is through the Internet. Try *www.fb-freizeitservice.de* or *www.flossfahrt.de* for two options. Parties don't come cheap, and this is no exception with individual prices ranging from Euro 100 to 125, depending upon services. Usually your fare includes bus transportation from Munich to your jumping off point (about a 30 minute bus trip), food, drink and entertainment, but be sure to ask when reserving.

Fluming on down the Isar River

Chapter 22

Holiday Treats:
Christmas, Traditions and Trinkets

No discussion of German life would be complete without some mention of Germany's holiday traditions, in particular, those of the Christmas season. Many of our own, most-loved and customary Christmas traditions originated in Germany, and cities and towns all across Germany transform themselves into enchanted villages, and shine with brilliance during the Christmas season.

Although many traditional Christmas symbols have seemingly been hijacked through commercialization, the spirit of Christmas is alive and well in Germany. Our modern day Santa Claus is derived from the legend of Saint Nikolaus, which was popularized by the Germans and the Dutch (hence both the names, St. Nick and Santa Claus, which in German, is pronounced 'Sankt Niklaus'). St. Nicholas was a prominent bishop who lived in the 7th century in what is modern-day Turkey. Having come from a wealthy family, St. Nikolaus had the means and the heart for gift-giving, and became known for his generosity. Through the centuries, his legend spread across Europe and firmly took hold in Germany. Although Christmas Eve is the main gift giving day of the Christmas season today, Germans still celebrate St. Nikolaus day, each December 6th, which marks St. Nikolaus's death, by giving small gifts to children.

In the early days, when the Church was trying to spread its word, it grabbed hold of the pagan winter festivals and made them their own by continuing to allow the people to revel in winter fun, but it now took on a significant religious meaning. That is why we today celebrate the birth of Christ in December. Similarly, the St. Nikolaus day was used by the Church to further its objectives. The Church thought it better that the Christchild be the one to bring gifts and hijacked the concept of gift-giving from St. Nikolaus day and moved it to the day of the birth of Christ. Here, once again, the Germans have bestowed upon us another Christmas tradition, that of Kris Kringle. Kris Kringle is derived from the German word for the Christchild, which is Christkind. For better or worse, the development of the modern version of Santa Claus and Christmas owes a debt of gratitude to the Germans.

The evergreen tree originated as a pagan symbol, but it was in Germany where the Christmas tradition took hold. Perhaps the biggest contribution to the Christmas tree tradition came from Martin Luther himself. Legend has it that one clear night around Christmas time, Luther was walking through the forest, looked up through the boughs of evergreen trees and saw the twinkling of the stars. The stars were so bright that they looked as if they were twinkling on the branches of the evergreens themselves. He then came upon the idea of putting candles on the Christmas tree, to resemble the stars, and that is why today we string white lights around the Christmas tree.

Germans celebrate Christmas with zeal and without the usual tackiness or kitsch. Nearly every city and town across Germany has its own *Christkindlesmarkt* (Christmas market). From the beginning of Advent until Christmas Eve (*Heilige Abend*), Germany's town squares and marketplaces are transformed into magical Christmas wonderlands. Colorfully-decorated, wooden stalls fill the squares, and are decked with white Christmas lights and decorated with wreaths and swags of pine. Vendors sell predominantly hand-carved, traditional wooden toys and decorations, such as Christmas pyramids and wooden nativity scenes. Stalls are filled with glass-blown, hand-painted Christmas tree ornaments, hand-crafted pewter ornaments and traditional Christmas woodcrafts. The Christmas markets have a convivial and friendly atmosphere which seems to overcome traditional German reserve. Evenings are the most special time to visit because the people congregate to buy gifts, take in the Christmas spirit, enjoy the Christmas decorations and share a drink or two while milling around. The drink of choice is *Glühwein*, ("glowing wine") which is a spiced or mulled red wine served with cinnamon sticks. It is so-called because the wine is heated to keep you warm while outside, and "glows" from the shining Christmas lights. The perfect accompaniment to *Glühwein* is a piece of Stollen or spicy gingerbread. Even if you are shopping at the Christmas market, the atmosphere is devoid of much of the usual Christmas hustle and bustle, and the Christmas spirit comes alive at the markets as friends and strangers share a few minutes of stress-free conversation and a drink or two to help ring in the season. The most famous *Christkindlesmarkt* are in Nuremberg, Munich, Köln, Augsburg, and Stuttgart, but you'll find them in nearly every town, and there is something special and cozy about the smaller ones.

Conclusion:
So long♪, farewell♪, auf Wiedersehen♪, Good-bye♪

As you've no doubt come to appreciate, Germany is a fascinating place with an enormous variety of cultural, social, economic and leisure time offerings. While some of the traditional stereotypes of Germans as a beer-drinking and sausage-eating people hold true and are quite essential to the fabric of being German, there is more to the Germans than meets the eye. By scratching the surface and getting beyond clichéd stereotypes, I hope you have begun to discover the Germans that you never knew existed.

In many ways, Germans are a complex people with seemingly inconsistent traits co-existing: serious, but fun-loving, reserved yet open, conservative on the one-hand and surprisingly liberal and progressive on the other. In their own right Germans really are crazy, but it is in an endearing sort of way. Most visitors to Germany often miss the opportunity to really experience the people and a culture because they are caught up in the beautiful architecture and landscape as they are whisked from place to place. For sure, the physical wonders of the country influence, and have been influenced by the people, but that is just one way of getting to know a place. The other is to learn about the people and what makes them unique, and then participate in some of the daily activities that really let's you get to know them and their culture.

I hope that ***Those Crazy Germans!*** has opened your eyes to the wonders of the German culture and that you've gotten some insight as to how they work and play, wine and dine, and think and act. Some things German may have surprised or even perplexed you, but you now have the inside scoop on Germany. With that, I hope that you set off to Germany to get your own *crazy* impressions and wish you a fun, enlightening and enriching trip. *Gute Reise!*

About the Author

Steve Somers is a self-proclaimed Germanophile. A lover of (nearly) all things German, Steve has been fascinated with Germany since his college days when he first began studying the German language. Steve has studied, worked and lived in Germany and traveled the country extensively, including places usually only frequented by Germans themselves. When not dreaming of Germany, Steve is professionally employed in the finance arena, having held a variety of corporate financial positions and earned the Chartered Financial Analyst (CFA) designation. Steve did his undergraduate work at Lehigh University and graduate work at Villanova University. He resides in suburban Philadelphia with his wife, Danielle and two children.

The author (center) with two of the crazier Germans he has known

Made in the USA
Lexington, KY
28 September 2011